Critical Guides to German Texts

1 G

Students and External Readers	Staff & Research Students
DATE DUE FOR RETURN	**DATE OF ISSUE**
12. MAR 86 3921	30. 08. 88
12. MAR 86 89 XXXXX	XX 10 X
	14 12 XXX
25. 06. 86 20. 03. 89	
08. 10. 8 XXXXXX	
08. 20 XXXXX	
09. 03. 8 9. 03. 89 XXXXXX	N.B. All books must be returned for the Annual Inspection in June
24. 06. 87 29. 06. 89	

Any book which you borrow remains your responsibility until the loan slip is cancelled

Critical Guides to German Texts

EDITED BY MARTIN SWALES

GRASS

Die Blechtrommel

Noel L. Thomas

Professor of German
University of Salford

Grant & Cutler Ltd
1985

© Grant & Cutler Ltd
1985
ISBN 0 7293 0219 9

303584

I.S.B.N. 84-599-0744-9
DEPÓSITO LEGAL: V. 1.145 - 1985

Printed in Spain by
Artes Gráficas Soler, S.A., Valencia
for
GRANT & CUTLER LTD
11 BUCKINGHAM STREET, LONDON W.C.2

Contents

Prefatory Note

The page numbers in brackets in this text refer to pages of *Die Blechtrommel* in the paperback edition (Sonderausgabe) published by Luchterhand, Darmstadt and Neuwied, 1981, and of *Der Butt* in the Luchterhand edition of 1977. Other references, indicated in brackets by italicised figures, are to the numbered items in the Select Bibliography.

In the course of writing this study I have been much indebted to Professor Angus Easson for reading and commenting upon the first draft, to Professor Martin Harris for his encouragement and to Professor Martin Swales for keeping a vigilant and helpful eye on my efforts. Furthermore I am most grateful for considerable secretarial assistance from the Department of Modern Languages at Salford University and to my wife for checking the text and the proofs. Finally I should like to acknowledge the kindness of John Benjamin's Publishing Company in allowing me to reprint in part sections from my book *The Narrative Works of Günter Grass, a Critical Interpretation*, which was published originally in 1982.

Introduction

When in 1959 *Die Blechtrommel* was first published it burst onto the literary scene like a bombshell, occasioning loud cries of horror, disgust, enthusiasm and admiration, according to the individual attitude of the critic concerned. Hans Magnus Enzensberger was quick to point out the uniqueness of Grass and of his first novel: 'Dieser Mann ist ein Störenfried, ein Hai im Sardinentümpel, ein wilder Einzelgänger in unserer domestizierten Literatur, und sein Buch ist ein Brocken wie Döblins *Berlin Alexanderplatz*, wie Brechts *Baal*, ein Brocken, an dem Rezensenten und Philologen mindestens ein Jahrzehnt lang zu würgen haben, bis es reif zur Kanonisation oder zur Aufbahrung im Schauhaus der Literaturgeschichte ist' (*6*). Enzensberger was unduly optimistic in quoting ten years as the minimum period of time which critics and academics would require in order to come to terms with the novel. The process of digestion is still under way and until digestion is complete, canonisation or storage still belongs to a somewhat remote future. Theories abound as to how the novel should be approached and how it should be interpreted, but no one single interpretation provides the ultimate truth. One has rather the impression that each new venture into the still partially uncharted interior of the novel complements but does not necessarily invalidate other previous pronouncements.

1. The Film of Die Blechtrommel

The production of Volker Schlöndorff's film of *Die Blechtrommel*, twenty years after the publication of the novel, allows a new approach to the novel and permits us to re-emphasise some of the statements which Grass himself has made and which sometimes are partially or completely ignored by those who seek to reduce the novel to a single, all-embracing formula. In comparing film and novel we shall also become aware of the correctness of Hans Magnus Enzensberger's response to the novel dating from the year 1959. What is more important, however, is that in relating the film to the novel, the distinctive qualities of the two artistic products may emerge with greater clarity. Before commencing this comparison it is worth recalling that Grass had confidence in Schlöndorff's capacity to adapt material in keeping with the aesthetics of the film director: 'Erst, als ich merkte, daß der Schlöndorff in der Lage ist, die Syntax des Schriftstellers, den Periodenbau des Schriftstellers in die Optik der Kamera zu übersetzen, da war die Sache für mich geklärt' (*22*, p.24). As a result of such confidence he felt justified in accepting Schlöndorff as a director who could convert the novel into a film.

One of the fundamental differences between the novel and the film is the change in narrative perspective. In the novel Oskar writes his memoirs in the years from 1952 to 1954 and in so doing covers the lives of his immediate ancestors and the thirty years of his own life (from September 1924 to September 1954). Oskar tells the story of himself, the child who at the age of three consciously refuses to enter the adult world, and accordingly contrives to cause an accident, a fall down some cellar steps, which arrests his growth. Oskar pretends to view the world through the eyes of a three-year-old child: his intellectual faculties remain unimpaired but he ceases to grow physically. The narrative perspective acquires a further complication by the fact that Oskar writes his life-story as an inmate of a lunatic asylum, having been confined there because he is suspected of murder. The opening sentence of the novel casts its shadow over the whole narrative:

> Zugegeben: ich bin Insasse einer Heil- und Pflegeanstalt, mein Pfleger beobachtet mich, läßt mich kaum aus dem Auge... (p.9)

In the film this qualification does not exist. The author, director and scriptwriter were in agreement that the situation of the narrator should be sacrificed: 'Es hätte sonst eine ständige Rückblende gegeben, umständlich und dreimal um die Ecke; was man mit einem Semikolon beim Schreiben machen kann, wird im Film umständlich' (*22*, p.23). This change in the position of the narrator is the basic difference between the film and the novel. In addition, there is the obvious fact that film and novel are two different artistic media. In the film everything is viewed initially through the eyes of the child, as though he were experiencing the events at the time. The viewer is presented with a series of tableaux or episodes with Oskar acting as commentator, 'doch nicht um Informationen zu geben, sondern um seine Gedanken zu sich und dem Geschehen zu formulieren' (*22*, p.38). As the film proceeds, the voice of Oskar as commentator intervenes less and less and the episodes are presented without the narrative mediator and with the characters speaking for themselves.

In the novel many of the interpretative difficulties which the reader experiences stem from the fact that an apparent madman recapitulates the past from the perspective of a child. The alienation effect which is thus produced coupled with the total amorality of the narrative viewpoint makes it virtually impossible for the reader to identify himself with Oskar or with any of the characters in the novel. In the film, however, orientation is much easier, for, as Schlöndorff maintains, the viewer can identify himself with Oskar (*22*, p.24). The possibility of our projecting ourselves into the situation of Oskar is enhanced by the fact that Oskar is portrayed as a child, and not as a dwarf.

Both Schlöndorff and Grass were of the opinion that Oskar should be portrayed as a child and Grass himself went so far as to maintain that the difficulties which would-be film directors experienced in assessing *Die Blechtrommel* originated in their misunderstanding the character of Oskar: 'Es gab ja große Schwierigkeiten in den Jahren davor bei den Leuten, die *Die Blechtrommel* verfilmen wollten. Sie gingen immer davon aus — das ist auch durch einen Teil der Literaturkritik mit verursacht —, sie sprachen immer von einem häßlichen Zwerg, von einem Gnom. Dabei macht das Buch deutlich: es ist ein Kind, das sein Wachstum eingestellt hat' (*22*, p.25). Furthermore, David Bennent, the child chosen by Schlöndorff to act the role of Oskar, is very attractive. Hence the credibility of Oskar in the film is not seriously in doubt, in the way that Oskar in the novel quickly brands himself as a thoroughly unreliable narrator. This is not to say that the viewer projects himself into the situation of Oskar as he shatters glass, either in the sitting-room or from the 'Stockturm', but rather that we can comprehend and enjoy Oskar's impishness, when, for example, he hangs the drum on the figure of Jesus in the 'Herz-Jesu-Kirche' or converts the Party rally into a festival of dance, and we can share the grief of Oskar at the loss of his mother. At the same time it can scarcely be maintained that we have a clear-cut notion of Oskar as a character — his principal attribute is his childishness, the fact that he is a child and indulges in childish activities. His attachment to his drum is the clearest indication of this. As in the novel, Oskar is primarily a person through whose eyes we view a period of German history. By his very childishness Oskar cannot sit in judgement on that period of time which he exposes to our gaze. Oskar perceives an amoral world in the amoral and egocentric terms of a child. But the reader of the novel is aware not only of the vulnerability and animalism of the child but also of his sophistication.

In identifying ourselves with Oskar, we can share in his grief at the destruction and loss of his native city — the film covers the first two books of the novel and ends with the train departing for the West with its load of refugees. The child who yearns to remain a child loses the place in which his childhood was spent.

A number of critics — though not Hans Magnus Enzensberger — seem to ignore the historical fact which forms the core of the novel and obviously of the film, i.e. the expulsion of the Germans from Danzig. The film emerges quite clearly as a lament and it ends with a painful sense of loss and deprivation. This effect is achieved largely because of what is presented visually by the camera, but also because we share in Oskar's sorrow. In seeing the film we are reminded of Enzensberger's statement about the novel: 'In der Tat ist *Die Blechtrommel* unter anderm auch ein historischer Roman aus dem zwanzigsten Jahrhundert, eine Saga der untergegangenen Freien Stadt Danzig, eine poetische Rettung jener kleinen Welt, in der Deutsche und Polen, Juden und Kaschuben zusammenlebten, vor dem Vergessenwerden' (6).

This quotation also allows one to draw conclusions about the nature of the German guilt. We are made to understand why Oskar is forced to leave his place of birth. The film shows most emphatically how the community of Danzig was systematically destroyed from within by the Germans. On the screen we see how Sigismund Markus, the Jew, is forcefully evicted from the cemetery where Anna Matzerath's funeral is taking place, we witness the German attack on the Polish Post Office and the breakdown of communication between the two national groups, and we are spectators at the *Kristallnacht* when Jewish shops and synagogues are set ablaze and when Sigismund Markus, Oskar's supplier of drums, commits suicide. Before Oskar and the remnants of his family depart for the West, his grandmother complains that the Kashubes, being neither German nor Poles, get it in the neck from both sides. The Germans shatter the community of Danzig. What happens in the microcosm of Oskar's native city happens elsewhere in Germany and in Europe. The Germans burden themselves with guilt. Oskar feels the need to be guilty and, in accordance with need and fashion, he indulges in the fantasy of having murdered mother, uncle, girl-friend (Roswitha Raguna) and father. The cinema audience cannot take such childish extravaganzas as seriously as do many readers when they see Oskar's confessions in black and white. The film allows one to gain at least some insight into what Grass has in mind when, in talking of Oskar, he refers to 'seine fingierte Schuld' and 'seine wirklichen Verschuldungen' (*8*, p.18). The theme of guilt is one which occupies a central position in the Danzig trilogy and throughout all Grass's narrative works, and one to which we shall return shortly.

The film constitutes a historical survey as seen through the eyes of a child, as commentator and, increasingly as the film progresses, as protagonist. It consists of a series of episodes which achieve a greater visual impact than their equivalents in the novel, but clearly cannot attain that level of subtlety and complexity which Oskar's highly sophisticated narrative performance displays. The film appears to be more realistic than the novel, whereas the novel can draw on elements of fantasy which are not at the disposal of the film and, by intermingling fantasy and reality, can achieve a greater range of associations and hence of implications than is the case with the film. Even though the episodes in the film may be regarded as a sequence of tableaux, the film is forced, for reasons of condensation, to reduce the extent of the imagery which makes such a major contribution to the total impact of the novel. Above all, the sacrifice of the narrator's position produces a simplified viewpoint, less ambivalence and ambiguity, and allows at least some identification between the viewer and Oskar, the commentator within the film. However, the total impact which the film achieves is not dissimilar, if one disregards the problems associated with the narrative perspective, from that which is achieved by the novel. Like the novel, the film of *Die Blechtrommel* is a lament which contains within it a critique of Germany's social and political behaviour.

Describing the film of *Die Blechtrommel* as a historical survey must not divert attention from the fact that the film — and the novel — do not deal with monumental history but with the history of banal petit-bourgeois circles in Danzig before the war. It is the world of the private individual that is being described. The pattern which the historian tries to impose upon the world of political events is absent from the world of the 'Kleinbürger' which Grass explores. As one might expect, the viewpoint of the child excludes him from the realm of monumental history. What

is especially frightening about the petit-bourgeois milieu is that
violence and animalism dominate it just as much as they do the
sphere of National Socialism. The attitudes of the petit
bourgeois inform even the upper strata of society where the
decision-making reputedly takes place. The 'kleinbürgerlich'
environment provides the nutrient medium for the Nazi
ideology. Throughout the film the audience witnesses a series of
violent actions: Oskar commits an act of grievous bodily harm
on himself by throwing himself down the cellar steps, the
children force a nauseating soup on him, Markus is evicted from
the cemetery, the Danzig synagogue is set ablaze, the Jewish toy
dealer commits suicide and the Polish Post Office is attacked.
Even the birth of Oskar is presented as a violent eruption, and
his acts of shattering glass are Oskar's reaction to the use of
physical force against himself and his drum. Violence in the
private sphere is a prelude to violence in the public sphere. There
is an escalation of brutality within the film — and within the
first two books of the novel — with an increasing interaction
between the private and the public spheres. The climax — logical
in terms of the violence which precedes it — is the shooting of
Matzerath and the eviction of the Germans from Danzig. The
escalation of cruelty in the film is accompanied by an increasing
lovelessness and physicality of the sexual relationships depicted
in the film, whether this be between Agnes and Jan Bronski,
Maria and Oskar or Maria and Matzerath. Unrequited love
degenerates into Oskar's attempting to assault Maria with a pair
of scissors. This sordid view of history is unsettling and untidy
and does not accord with the nominally structured nature of
monumental history. It achieves its horrifying impact, not by
interconnecting social, political and historical facts and
imposing a pattern upon them, but by the selection of detail and
by highlighting characteristic attitudes and behaviour.

The explosive immediacy of the film is enhanced by the fact
that the commentator and principal protagonist is a child. Oskar
surveys his surroundings with naive and unprejudiced eyes, and
his incredulity throws into relief the viciousness of the age
through which he is living. His defencelessness in a merciless
world also serves to accentuate the horrific nature of his

environment. The audience's experience of Oskar's world is more direct in the film than it is in the novel. Less interpretative dexterity is demanded of the viewer than of the reader. This is occasioned by the fact that Oskar's voice and the film camera share the narrative, and especially in the opening stages of the film. As David Head observes,[1] Schlöndorff even goes so far as to emphasise the partnership of voice and camera by having Oskar speak through a diaphragm. The division of labour between voice and camera, with the camera ultimately assuming the dominant role, diminishes the sophistication and the many-sidedness of the narration and reduces the stature of the narrator. The shift in emphasis from the linguistic to the visual also diminishes the quality of the irony, which is a constant feature of the novel's narrative style. The visual presentation has the effect of lessening ambiguity though this is not to say that irony and satire cannot be conveyed by the juxtaposition of disparate elements, as, for example, when nuns hold aloft a banner bearing the words 'Glaube Hoffnung Liebe' against the background of a burning synagogue.

Not only does the film dispense with the narrative perspective of the novel but, as has already been suggested, it alters in a quite fundamental way the character of the narrator. In the novel the narrator emerges as a volatile and unreliable witness. As a narrative device rather than a fully fledged character, he is a strange synthetic creation. As such Oskar both presents and distorts the history of his time. The unstable narrative con-coction which is thereby produced leaves the reader insecure and bereft of orientation. Oskar is not a critic of his time, the mask of the child prevents that. In any case he is victim and victimiser and he is too whimsical and unpredictable to maintain a con-sistent and coherent viewpoint. Hence Oskar does not sit in judgement on his age; but his naive and unprejudiced gaze does uncover the moral confusion of his petit-bourgeois milieu. Moreover, by implication he lays bare the sordid and brutal manœuvrings at a higher level. The unhinged mind narrating

[1] David Head, 'Volker Schlöndorff's *Die Blechtrommel* and the *"Literatur-verfilmung"* Debate', in *German Life and Letters*, Vol.XXXVI, No.4, July 1983, pp.347-67.

through a veil of irony shows the unhinged nature of the world in which he is living. His narrative is strangely revealing. But precisely because he does not sit in judgement, he does not bring to his task a set of criteria by which his revelations could be assessed. In spite of this, 'das Pandämonium des Günter Grass', a description which has been negatively applied to *Hundejahre*, does highlight in incisive and painful manner the pandemonium of German history.

The film is a simplified version of the novel, not only because of the change in narrative perspective and in the character of the narrator, the shift from the linguistic to the visual, the reduced imaginative content, and the diminished impact of the imagery, but also because it stops short at the year 1945. In other words the film is unable to convey the impression of historical continuity which stretches across the great divide of 1945, linking together the period of National Socialism and the post-war era. The differences between film and novel help us to isolate the distinctive features of the novel, that is, the narrative perspective, the narrative skill, the imagery, and the chronological framework. Let us now turn to an analysis of the novel and concern ourselves in particular with these four aspects as well as with the theme of guilt. We shall also need to pay attention to the linguistic aspects of the novel and to questions relating to irony, satire and the grotesque. We shall need to show both the problematic nature of Oskar Matzerath's narrative and the extent to which (and the ways in which) Grass makes that narrative offensively, painfully revelatory.

2. Narrative Perspective

In discussing the narrative perspective in *Die Blechtrommel* it is useful to remind ourselves of the remarks which Grass himself has made on the topic, to which Kurt Lothar Tank refers in his book (see *23*). Grass describes how he had originally written a cycle of poems entitled *Der Säulenheilige*. It tells of a young man who suddenly gives up his career as a mason and becomes a stylite. Grass goes on to say that Oskar ultimately takes up an equally eccentric viewpoint: 'Aus Oskar ist dann später ein umgekehrter Säulenheiliger geworden. Es erwies sich, daß der Mann auf der Säule zu statisch ist, um ihn Prosa sprechen zu lassen, und deswegen ist Oskar von der Säule herabgestiegen. Er blieb nicht bei der normalen Größe, sondern ist noch ein bißchen mehr an die Erde gegangen und hat dann einen Blickwinkel, der dem Blickwinkel des Säulenheiligen entgegengesetzt ist' (*23*, p.59). It is clear that Oskar, the narrator, is intended to view human affairs from an unusual angle. This perspective allows Grass to describe human beings and events in a way in which adults would not normally perceive them. In the same conversation with Bienek (see *23*), Grass comments upon the advantages which stem from the fact that his main figure ceases to grow at the age of three and yet from his birth onwards possesses the intelligence and clear-sightedness of the adult with all his faults and false speculations. He states that Oskar is later not regarded as an adult by those with whom he comes into contact, but always remains 'der Dreikäsehoch', the 'enfant terrible', the urchin who cannot belong to the adult world. From this eccentric point of view Oskar is able to play the role of observer and narrator, viewing not only the people who surround him but the whole epoch in a manner which Grass describes as being 'von unten nach oben'. It is important to note that Oskar is described as 'seeing' the world around him: there is no suggestion of his judging or criticising events and people —

something that one could scarcely expect of a child in any case.

The narrative perspective is complicated still further by another factor. Idris Parry[2] reminds us of a fundamental truth about fiction when he says that 'what we are reading is not actually happening, but is being recalled and put together for our benefit by a sentient human being' (p.102). This we automatically accept, perhaps almost unconsciously. In *Die Blechtrommel* the past is certainly being conjured up, structured and restructured. However, it is being recalled by a much flawed sentient human being, in other words by someone who admits that he is the inmate of a mental asylum. This huge qualification, as we have already stated earlier, is erected like a warning sign at the beginning of the novel, indicating in no uncertain terms that an unreliable narrator is at work. This first sentence of *Die Blechtrommel*, one of the few certainties in the novel, affects our assessment of each individual piece of information with which Oskar provides us. We are constantly forced to pose the question: whether a given statement may be considered valid in view of the fact that Oskar might be a madman. Oskar does not describe himself as being insane, he contents himself with the observation that he is the inmate of a lunatic asylum. Oskar's introductory remark contains within it a second qualification; from it the reader gathers that the narrator is describing his own life after the passage of what is in many cases a considerable amount of time. As can be seen by examining the time-scale within the novel, Oskar is not presenting us with a diary written day by day and recounting the events of the immediate past. The passage of time, we must presume, will have blurred some of the details and perhaps even have allowed imagination to reconstruct the past. We have to be satisfied with Oskar's pious hope that he has an accurate memory. Ambiguity, ambivalence and disorientation reign supreme: the reader has to contend with what is to all intents and purposes a double perspective as an apparent or real madman recounts the events of his life through the eyes of a child. The 'terrible fluidity of self-revelation', to use Henry James's

---

[2] Idris Parry, 'Aspects of Günter Grass's Narrative Technique', in *Forum for Modern Language Studies*, Vol.III, No.2, 1967, pp.99-114.

description of the first-person narrative, is complete.

Yet even the term 'self-revelation' is incorrect when applied to Oskar, for the narrator does not reveal himself. Oskar does not grant us any real insight into his own personality and we have little or no understanding of his motivation, apart from the fact that he refuses to assume responsibility, opting out of any moral obligations towards others. Oskar's unreliability as a conveyor of information is an indication of the fact that he is estranged from himself, and this is reinforced in a number of ways: his craving to return to the prenatal state is a sign of his alienation from the present whilst at the same time being a comment on the state of the world and his attitude to it; his attachment to his drum is also indicative of his fractured relationship to reality; the existence of 'two souls fighting within his breast', the Oskar who acts and the Oskar who observes, the one who feels and the one who thinks, such divisions are a sign of the narrator's schizophrenia. His attachment to the mask of the child, his assumed pose of innocence, his delight in falsehood and prevarication, his destruction of truth, all suggest that he has not broken away from the seductive world of childish — and romantic — inwardness. Oskar does not succeed in emerging from infantile subjectivism, in making the journey from childhood to adulthood, and at the same time exploits the possibilities of feigned innocence in order to prevent his transition from inwardness to maturity. So fragmented is Oskar's personality that he does not emerge as a character. His eccentric, highly imaginative viewpoint is a sign of the individual who has never acquired a focal point for his existence and is hence subject to the centrifugal forces at work within himself and within society. He is a *persona* and not a personality.

As a *persona*, as an inscrutable sentient human being, Oskar acts solely as an observer in many instances throughout the course of the novel without participating actively in the events which are taking place. From his vantage point under the table, for example, Oskar is able to observe, 'von unten nach oben', the manœuvres of his uncle's foot during the game of *Skat* (p.54). This is the classic instance of Oskar, the child, exploiting his unique perspective to the full. Oskar is the willing or unwilling witness of other equally interesting scenes, and in all such instances he brings an unprejudiced eye to the scenes which he witnesses. His descriptive powers are not inhibited by any form of censorship. His attitude is not affected by the religious or sexual taboos of the adult and it would be true to say that he is equally open-minded about the subject of death. As Enzensberger states, 'Grass jagt nicht, wie Henry Miller, hinter dem Tabu her: er bemerkt es einfach nicht' (*6*, p.221). Oskar is thus able to enjoy a freedom of expression which the adult observer could not enjoy at all. Much of the humour of the novel — albeit frequently of a black variety and unfolding within the context of the grotesque — stems from the fact that our narrator approaches adult affairs in such an unprejudiced manner. He is not afraid to survey the totality of the human experience. This totality includes smells, some of which are obnoxious, sexual practices which may be disagreeable, and blasphemy, and none of these experiences accords with the expectations of bourgeois orderliness. Oskar, as may be expected, does not engage in any false moralising; as a child, or a madman assuming the guise of a child, he can adopt a completely neutral attitude to the happenings which take place around him — or took place, since Oskar is conjuring up the events of the past. Oskar is absolved of the requirement which is automatically imposed upon a thirty-year-old, that of assessing the past in terms of the adult. Such assessment inevitably involves a moral evaluation, the statement that this is right or that is wrong; or it involves slanting the 'facts' in keeping with the pattern associated with a given philosophical or ideological attitude. Oskar can dispense with such encumbrances. He presents us with the details of the scenes which unfold, retrospectively, before his eyes though, of course, the 'facts' he submits to us are the 'facts' as seen through the eyes of a child or a madman. They are tinged by the limitations, or limitlessness, of the mentality of the child or the madman. Oskar recreates the past, or attempts to do so, with the qualification that through Oskar we receive an eccentric perception of the event, which lacks the familiar perspective of stable narrative writing.

As a result of this perspective it is possible to find a large number of statements and actions in the novel which express the attitude of the child. When, for example, Oskar visits the opera, he plunges the theatre into darkness because he thinks the spotlight is blinding the singer (p.90). The brutality of the *Kristallnacht* is described in the terms of the child who is baffled by the nature of the events which he sees happening. The whole chapter is punctuated by the phrase 'Es war einmal...', which gives it the incomprehensible flavour of a savage nursery tale (pp.159-66). During the defence of the Polish Post Office Oskar cannot understand why the adults are not bothered about his drum (p.179). Many of Oskar's statements and actions are amusing because they are those of a naive, unprejudiced, self-centred child. He is concerned solely with his own interests and desires. Hence when Kobyella is wounded, Oskar describes this occurrence in the following terms: 'da hatte sich eine Granate einen Riesenspaß erlaubt' (p.190). Oskar's pronouncements may be interpreted often on two, if not three, levels: they may stem from the naturalness and simplicity of the child who is baffled by adult affairs or, what is more likely, from the deranged mind of an adult who has successfully projected himself into the mentality of a child or, alternatively, they may be based on the playfulness and the tongue-in-cheek attitude of the person who is acting the role of the child, stating on many occasions the opposite of what he believes. Such an ironic point of view allows the author to describe the events of our age in a detached manner, prevents him from becoming either judge or prosecutor.

Amidst so much ambiguity and ambivalence the reader often finds himself bewildered. He is disconcerted by the ever changing fluidity of the narrative and of Oskar's pronouncements. He feels unsure of himself and lacks confidence in his capacity to come to any firm conclusions. The narrative perspective engenders doubt in his mind: doubt about himself and doubt about Oskar, the source of his so-called information. The reader scarcely knows when to take Oskar seriously: the narrator's humour, irony and impishness form a barrier which makes it all the more difficult to know Oskar as a person. It is not merely the drum which separates him from the adult world but also the virtually impenetrable wall of derision, irony and doubt. Oskar's ironic perspective leads to a debunking of political happenings and attitudes, often because his mind interconnects details in a childish, inconsequential and often irreverent manner: he links, for example, the defeat of the German army in North Africa with Kurt's recovery from whooping cough (p.261). The ironic pose characterises many of Oskar's observations about history and politics. His comment on the partition of Poland is a good example of this:

> Der Friede zu Oliva. — Wie hübsch und friedlich das klingt. Dort bemerkten die Großmächte zum erstenmal, daß sich das Land der Polen wunderbar fürs Aufteilen eignet (p.328).

The same sham seriousness is in evidence when Oskar refers to Marshal Rokossovsky's arrival in Danzig:

> Der erinnerte sich beim Anblick der heilen Stadt an seine großen internationalen Vorgänger, schoß erst einmal alles in Brand, damit sich jene, die nach ihm kamen, im Wiederaufbau austoben konnten (p.329).

The superficially humorous tone conceals an underlying bitterness and despair, which, if it had to be categorised, is more the expression of the mind of an adult than that of a child. Such a point of view, whether this be the naivety of a child or the irony of an adult, allows a detached treatment of the events concerned, permits the reader to gain the necessary distance from an epoch in which he himself may be involved too emotionally, and demolishes all preconceived judgements.

There are other events in the novel in which Oskar actively participates but in which he nevertheless still preserves his dominant role as the naive or ironic observer. During the course of Oskar's lessons at the hands of Gretchen Scheffler it is just as important for the reader to be able to observe Gretchen and Agnes reacting to Rasputin as it is for us to realise the nature of Oskar's upbringing. Oskar is the witness of this scene which is meant to have a general validity, at least with reference to the German context, and which we as the readers view through the eyes of Oskar. In the chapter entitled 'Schaufenster' (pp.99-108), Oskar cuts holes in the glass of shop-windows and thereby presents himself, and us, with the opportunity of watching how others react to temptation. In 'Glaube Hoffnung Liebe' the bewildered child tells of his reaction to the events of the *Kristall-nacht*. Once again Oskar acts as the observer — though his is a flawed vision — and in this instance he certainly does not take part in the happenings at all. In his post-war career Oskar apparently adapts himself to the demands of the art students and in this sense seems to be fashioned by them. Hence the 'Madonna 49' says as much about the guilt-ridden complexes of the students and their teacher as it does about Oskar. The situation is clearer still with regard to Oskar's activities as a drummer in the Onion Cellar and his later tours of West Germany. Oskar certainly assumes an active role on these occasions but it is the tearful breast-beating of the guests which claims our attention and which is exposed to ridicule. And we are told furthermore that they are intended to represent West German society. Oskar is in effect the fractured medium through which the activities of others may be scrutinised. The figure of Oskar is the device which enables West German society to be held up to our gaze.

Yet merely to describe Oskar as an observer is to oversimplify the situation. We are constantly reminded that he is a thoroughly untrustworthy witness. He himself has no illusions about his unreliability. Having located himself in a lunatic asylum he emphasises that he indulges in telling lies in the process of relating the events of his life to Bruno Münsterberg, his mental nurse:

> Liebgewonnen habe ich ihn, erzähle dem Gucker hinter der Tür, sobald er mein Zimmer betritt, Begebenheiten aus meinem Leben, damit er mich trotz des ihn hindernden Guckloches kennenlernt. Der Gute scheint meine Erzählungen zu schätzen, denn sobald ich ihm etwas vorgelogen habe, zeigt er mir, um sich erkenntlich zu geben, sein neuestes Knotengebilde (p.9).

Oskar thus emphasises his delight in falsehood from the outset. The desire to pretend, the child's inclination to lose itself in the inner world of imagination and to ignore the dividing line between the real and the fictional, the momentary wish to pull somebody's leg — whether it be Münsterberg's or the reader's — all this soon manifests itself in Oskar's life. Even on the day of his birth Oskar would have us believe that he plays at being a baby (p.37). Acting as a child, playing a role, becomes a permanent feature of Oskar's behaviour. Throughout the novel, Oskar constantly refers to his need to erect a façade of pretence and deceit between himself and grown-ups. A person who has elevated make-believe into an essential principle of his life cannot be considered as a reliable narrator whose judgement can be trusted and whose statements are always in focus. Oskar is to be regarded rather as a narrative device or ironical viewpoint than as a person whose character can be understood in psychological terms and whose statements give us insight into his personality. Jochen Rohlfs explains the role of the narrator in the following way: 'Dabei kommt es Grass weniger darauf an, den Erzähler selbst menschlich-überzeugend zu gestalten, als ihm vielmehr eine Perspektive abzugewinnen, aus der das Zeitgeschehen realistischer als gemeinhin in Geschichtsbüchern dargestellt werden kann' (*1*, p.52).

The presence of dissembling, that is meant to be seen through, is, it has often been claimed, a fundamental element in irony (see *15*, p.26). Since Oskar is telling his story from an assumed point of view, pretence can be said to be one of Oskar's basic principles. He tries to observe the world through the innocent or naive eyes of the child, or from the point of view of the madman. Grass, however, allows Oskar to be only partly successful in his attempts at disguise, and hence a contrast emerges between what the narrator appears to be saying and what the situation might well be. We are certainly made aware that Oskar's world of make-believe is not to be taken at face value. We know, in other words, that Oskar does not present us with a true picture of reality because he intermingles fact and fiction. We are not, however, made aware of those objective criteria by which we could gain an insight into the character of

Oskar or into the nature of the reality which he is overtly attempting to conceal. Only in this negative sense is it possible to speak of a contrast in the novel between appearance and reality, a contrast which, according to D.C. Muecke, is a basic feature of irony. Admittedly the framework of political and historical references constitutes a stabilising factor within the novel, provides, along with the reader's knowledge of the period of history concerned, a set of verifiable external relationships, and hence forms a link with the reality of the time. As would be expected, the irony is meant to be detected. As D.C. Muecke asserts, 'the half-concealment is part of the ironist's artistic purpose and the detection and appreciation of the camouflage is a large part of the reader's pleasure' (*15*, pp.52-53). The other characteristics of irony which Muecke mentions in his book can easily be found in the style of *Die Blechtrommel*: a comic element, an element of detachment, and what he refers to as an aesthetic element (*15*, p.48).

In a sense it is true to say that the reader is presented with two levels of irony in *Die Blechtrommel*. He knows that there is a supreme godlike ironist in the background and by turning to the cover of the book he learns that the ironist in question bears the name of Günter Grass. The author interposes a narrator between himself and the reader, and leaves the latter without any instruction, direct or indirect, for understanding his creation. The reader is left to judge the characters and situations in the novel, unable to rely on the advice of its maker. Meanwhile Grass hands over the task of narrating to Oskar, who, as an ironist, is himself cast in the same mould as his creator, simulates innocence or madness and sees the world, revealed in all its starkness, through this glass of dissembling. Our only contact with reality in the novel, apart from the chronological framework of history, is through the troubled vision of Oskar, who makes it his purpose to deceive us, fortunately inconsistently, and perhaps on occasions he even deceives himself. We are hence confronted with the kind of situation which, according to Wayne C. Booth, readers face in coming to terms with the novels of Henry James. The latter, he tells us, 'fails to provide any theory relevant to one large segment of his own work — those stories narrated, whether in the first or third person, by a profoundly confused, basically self-deceived, or even wrong-headed or vicious reflector' (*2*, p.340). Grass similarly does not supply any theories, instructions or even hints for interpreting the statements of his narrator. Like Henry James, Günter Grass shrouds his narrator in ambiguity and ambivalence.

In his discussion of irony, D.C. Muecke claims that 'verbal irony is employed principally (i) as a rhetorical device — the ironist asserts a 'falsehood' knowing he can rely upon the listener to contradict it mentally by an indignant or amused counter-assertion, this counter-assertion with all its emphasis being the ironist's real meaning, (ii) as solemn foolery ..., (iii) as a weapon of satire, or, more broadly, in the interests of morality. As a satirist or moralist, the ironist may... present situational ironies particularly ironies of self-betrayal or incongruity' (*15*, p.63). All four types of irony may be found throughout the course of *Die Blechtrommel*. Satirical elements are present in all parts of the novel, though perhaps more especially in the third book in which Grass deals with the post-war period, e.g. in the chapter entitled 'Madonna 49' and 'Im Zwiebelkeller'. Günter Grass has been described as a satirist (see *10*) and Grass himself refers to the satiric element in his novel. Nevertheless, Wayne C. Booth's observation that extensive ambiguity in a novel will be paid for by a loss of satiric force is, I think, relevant in discussing *Die Blechtrommel* as a work of satire. Examples of solemn foolery, the pronouncements of the clown or of the impish child, abound throughout the novel and are placed like traps in the path of the critic who wishes to prod them in search of the elusive truth. In referring to irony as a rhetorical device Muecke touches upon one of the fundamental problems which arises in the analysis of *Die Blechtrommel*. It is clear from what has already been said that it is impossible for the reader to identify himself with the narrator or his characters and that there is a gulf between Oskar's set of values — or non-values — and those of the reader. In commenting upon the opening words of the novel Georg Just makes the following observation: ' "Identifikationsverweigerung" bzw. "Wertesystemkonflikt'' bezeichnet die Struktur dieses Textes' (*12*, p.33). In the same article he comes to the conclusion that the inadequacy of Oskar's actions provokes the reader into setting up his own criteria, examining the situation and considering what behaviour might have been appropriate: 'Die Inadäquatheit von Oskars Handeln gibt nicht Anweisung zu allegorischer Ausdeutung — Ergebnis einer solchen könnten immer nur willkürliche Spekulationen sein — sondern zur Reflektion der eigenen Einstellung. D.h. die Handlungsanweisung, die davon ausgeht, richtet sich nicht unmittelbar auf die damalige Situation: so und so hättest du handeln sollen, sondern an die Reflexion des Lesers: überleg dir, welches Handeln der damaligen Situation adäquat gewesen wäre, wenn (a) Oskars Handeln, (b) das Handeln der dargestellten Zeitgenossen — wenn auch auf verschiedenen Ebenen — als inadäquat gelten muß' (*12*, p.42). Georg Just is certainly correct in stating that *Die Blechtrommel* cannot be interpreted satisfactorily in allegorical terms, but this only confirms what Grass himself has said. Both Muecke and Just are analysing a similar situation in that both stress the importance of the reader's response: the reader is provoked into reacting against the narrator's actions and statements. George Just is rather too restrictive in stressing the idea that the reader should reflect on the characters' actions. For it is frequently the case that we are stimulated into formulating our own attitude as a counterweight to the narrator's attitude and pondering upon the totality of Oskar's behaviour, and of the German situation, especially when one bears in mind Grass's avowed intention: 'ich will nur die Strömungen der Zeit einfangen' (*3*, p.198). In approaching the novel the reader is thrust back upon himself, is dependent on his own resources, must provide his own criteria, for there are no guidelines within the novel; he must formulate his own response and come to his own conclusions. Irony, however, can take on various forms, as we have already seen. Furthermore, Oskar's dissembling, the pretence which is the basic ingredient of his ironic pose, may assume an equally wide range of forms: the narrator indulges in exaggeration, prevarication, flights of fancy, bravado, self-pity, melodrama, loss of perspective,

unrealistic statements, fibs, indeed downright lies and many
other tricks. Oskar twists and turns like an eel. The confidence
trickster is never still — one pose is rapidly supplanted by
another. His lack of seriousness constantly diverts attention
from himself. In addition Oskar draws comparisons between the
events and characters of his stories and the events and characters
in literary and religious contexts. Parody is yet another aspect of
the histrionics which Oskar enjoys so much. The narrator
produces a rich kaleidoscopic effect in order to preserve his
facelessness. In short, the reader must be as agile as the impostor
and no single, stock response can cope with the ever shifting
fluidity of Oskar's phantasmagoria.

3. Irony, Satire and the Grotesque

As has already been stated, all the four categories of irony to which Muecke refers (see *15*) are employed in the course of *Die Blechtrommel*. Examples of solemn foolery abound throughout the novel. After Oskar has described how his grandfather escaped from his pursuers by diving under the rafts, we read Gottfried Vittlar's analysis of the grandfather's behaviour:

> 'Dein Großvater unterschlug der Welt und seinem Enkelkind die Leiche, damit sich die Nachwelt und das Enkelkind noch lange mit ihm befassen mögen' (p.29).

In that the statement is a fantastic departure from reality, it may be regarded as an instance of solemn foolery, and it is at least declaimed in an ostensibly solemn, albeit theatrical manner. At the same time it contains a comic element and an element of religious parody, and in that it is dealing with the death of a person, there is equally a touch of the macabre in this comment. In short, a number of disparate elements are in evidence in this quotation, all are gathered together under the general umbrella of irony, and the reader is called upon to react to these various components simultaneously. It is scarcely to be wondered at that the reader, versatile though he may be in his range of reaction and his responsiveness, may well feel bewildered and disorientated.

To quote another example of solemn foolery, before Oskar's umbilical cord is severed, our hero indulges in speculation:

> Einsam und unverstanden lag Oskar unter den Glühbirnen, folgerte, daß das so bleibe, bis sechzig, siebenzig Jahre später ein endgültiger Kurzschluß aller Lichtquellen Strom unterbrechen werde, verlor deshalb die Lust, bevor dieses Leben unter den Glühbirnen anfing; und nur die in

Aussicht gestellte Blechtrommel hinderte mich damals,
dem Wunsch nach Rückkehr in meine embryonale Kopf-
lage stärkeren Ausdruck zu geben (p.37).

Reminiscent of Laurence Sterne's *Tristram Shandy*, an utterly
fantastic situation is described in a matter-of-fact, logical
manner and the reader is amused by the imaginative extra-
vaganza and the playful whimsicality of the narrator and his
author. The reader may react also to the underlying witticism
which draws a humorous parallel between 'Entschluß' (in the
previous sentence), 'folgerte' and 'Kurzschluß'. The short-
circuiting of human life, the interlinking of the non-human and
human spheres, will also elicit a smile from the reader. The
solemn foolery — or tomfoolery — provokes mainly an amused
response, that is, if one disregards the fact that the reader is
introduced — or reintroduced — to two of the dominant themes
in Oskar's life, the drum and the desire for retreat (the former
being in many cases the externalisation of the latter). The ironic
impish pretence of this passage may occasion only this one
reaction on the part of the reader. Nevertheless he still remains
disconcerted partly because he is predisposed to expect ambivalence, and he is quite likely to be unsure, certainly in the first
instance, of the significance of the drum and the embryonic head
position. The irony which inevitably inclines the reader to doubt
is accompanied by the urge to unravel the general meaning, to
discover, in other words, what intellectual or emotional reality
underlies the fantasy. Thus the common denominator in both
the passages we have cited has been the fact that the reader is
forced into a questioning attitude.

There are other contexts in which, at least initially, the
unsettling of the reader is more acute than in the preceding
example. Take, for instance, the first page of the novel, where
Oskar makes the following baffling claims:

Mein weißlackiertes metallenes Anstaltsbett ist also ein
Maßstab. Mir ist es sogar mehr: mein Bett ist das endlich
erreichte Ziel, mein Trost ist es und könnte mein Glaube
werden, wenn mir die Anstaltsleitung erlaubte, einige

Änderungen vorzunehmen: das Bettgitter möchte ich
erhöhen lassen, damit mir niemand mehr zu nahe tritt.

The bed as a yardstick seems incomprehensible as an idea if
detached from its context but, given the fact that Oskar rejects
Bruno's suggestion of colouring his knots red by insisting on the
undesirability of painting his bed any other colour than white, it
becomes acceptable as part of the fantastic continuity of
associations. One could dismiss the other descriptions of
Oskar's bed as extravagant overstatements of the pleasure he
gains from staying in bed. The reader has to wait until almost
the last chapter of the book before he learns that Oskar has
feigned madness, taken to the institutional bed to escape the
responsibilities of adulthood. In this sense the bed is for Oskar a
goal and source of comfort. The bathos involved in the reference
to raising the bedrail is a plunge from sublime exaggeration into
the commonplace whilst being at the same time a reminder of
Oskar's need to keep his fellow men and women at bay, in order
to protect himself against their intrusions and to preserve his
veneer of pretence. Reality and fantasy, the serious and the
comic, the obvious and the cryptic, all coexist in uneasy relationship. Each noun applied to the bed achieves a shock-effect and
jolts the reader into pondering upon its significance and
establishing meaningful patterns and interrelationships. As with
the other passages we have quoted, ambivalence reigns supreme.

Not infrequently solemn foolery is tinged with satire. When,
for example, the social democrat objects to an additional two
women and six children being assigned to the goods waggon he is
occupying, along with many others, on their journey westwards,
the Polish officer is quick to demolish any claims which a social
democrat might have to special treatment:

Aber der polnische Offizier, der den Transport leitete,
ohrfeigte ihn, als er nicht Platz machen wollte und gab in
recht fließendem Deutsch zu verstehen, daß er nicht wisse,
was das bedeute, Sozialdemokrat. Er habe sich während
des Krieges an verschiedenen Orten Deutschlands
aufhalten müssen, während der Zeit sei ihm das Wörtchen
Sozialdemokrat nie zu Gehör gekommen (p.348).

The officer's tongue-in-cheek rejection of the term 'social democrat' is a delightful piece of irony and is accompanied by the understatement of his having to stay in Germany during the war, thus concealing, though suggesting, that he might have been the inmate of a concentration camp or a 'Fremdarbeiter' or a prisoner of war. The assertion that he had never heard the 'Wörtchen' during his sojourn in Germany could be taken, given the probability of his restricted circumstances, as a virtual statement of fact though presented in exaggerated form, and yet there is the in-built suggestion that the Nazi regime had reduced the term to a state of non-existence. Thus the reader is confronted in this quotation with an ostensibly solemn piece of foolery to which he reacts in both an amused and in a deadly serious manner. Within the ironic framework of exaggeration and understatement we note the aggressive, almost savage comment on the circumstances of the Pole's internment, the Nazi regime and the resultant attitude. Such a context demands the active and total involvement of the reader and he has to produce simultaneously a range of reactions, one frequently in conflict with the other. He is called upon to assess the situation which is being described in the novel, whilst casting a wary eye on the narrator and/or author. At the same time he has to bring to the text a knowledge of the political and social circumstances of the time. He will be aware that the irony is meant to be detected and he will, as in this instance, derive pleasure from the detection and appreciation of the camouflage. If it is accepted that this particular quotation has a satiric thrust, the reader does not recognise the critical intent because of criteria which are stated or implied but because of the disparity between appearance and reality. Yet again, as with all aspects of Grass's style, the reader is forced back upon himself in his efforts to interpret the text. This passage illustrates the fundamental problem of irony: the reader is called upon to react against the surface meaning and assemble a secondary meaning from the hints which the author provides. Accordingly the reader can never be sure whether his response has followed the right path and whether the scale of his reaction is too restricted or too far-reaching.

One further and final example of solemn foolery illustrates another problem which arises in the analysis of irony and of satire, that is, the relationship between the comic and serious elements, whether the comic heightens the impact of the serious, the tragic or the horrific. During the defence of the Polish Post Office, for example, Oskar, Jan Bronski and Kobyella, the caretaker who has been fatally wounded, play *Skat* in the storeroom, until the death of Kobyella brings the game to an untimely end and Jan is forced to realise,

> daß es auf dieser Welt keinen dritten Mann für den Skat mehr gab. Da wurde es sehr still in dem Lagerraum für Briefsendungen. Auch draußen bequemte man sich zu einer ausgedehnten Gedenkminute für den letzten Skatbruder und dritten Mann (p.198).

The humour stems obviously from the fact that the minute's silence is held, not for the soldier Kobyella, who dies in the defence of Poland, but for the last *Skat* player, and it is enhanced by the silence and the mourning ostensibly being shared by the outside world, which, as we know, is inhabited by armoured scout cars, howitzers and flame-throwers. Words such as 'sich bequemen' and 'ausgedehnt' reinforce the ironic idea. The ironic is thus accompanied by the macabre and the horrific in a way which has much in common with the grotesque. If one considers the associations which have attached themselves to the game of *Skat* throughout the novel, then it will be apparent that the death of the last *Skat* player — and it is noteworthy that he is the last in the whole world — is emblematic of the final breakdown of human relationships between two national groups, for the game of *Skat* as played by Agnes and Alfred Matzerath and Jan Bronski was a sign that the two communities, the Polish and German, could still live in harmony. In this sense the tragic quality of Kobyella's death is accentuated, and thus the comic coexists with the tragic. As ever Günter Grass is double- if not treble-stopping, playing on two or more strings at the same time, and coalescing what would otherwise be entirely discrete elements. Grass's technique contributes to the

consternation of the reader, which is further intensified by the
need to unravel and identify the associations of the imagery
employed. In referring to a passage from Swift's *Modest
Proposal*, Philip Thomson speculates in his book on the
grotesque, 'whether the comic element does not in effect make
the whole thing even more shocking, even more difficult to
stomach' (*25*, p.5). Though we are not dealing with an extreme
manifestation of the grotesque in this quotation taken from *Die
Blechtrommel*, the same problem of interpretation does apply. It
seems to me that, as in the juxtaposition of comic and tragic
scenes in Shakespeare's plays, the coexistence of the comic and
of the tragic, which in the case of irony or satire is simultaneous,
enhances our appreciation of each element — and of their
interdependence.

The reader does not encounter Muecke's category of verbal
irony, that of the rhetorical device, in as much profusion as the
instances of solemn foolery, or, as we shall see later, as the
examples of satire. The fact that it does exist, however,
illustrates yet again the extent to which the narrative viewpoint,
though constant in that it stems from an attitude of dissembling,
finds its expression in a large number of different, even changing
forms, thus demanding a high degree of intellectual and
emotional agility — and for that matter quickness of response —
from the reader. As has already been stated, Muecke defines the
ironic rhetorical device as the stating of a 'falsehood' which
provokes the reader into producing a counter-assertion. The
counter-assertion, it is maintained, is then the ironist's real
meaning, though it seems to me that it is often no more than a
spirited negation of the original statement. Such a denial will be
accompanied by an appropriate mixture of amusement and
indignation, and since a 'falsehood' invariably stimulates
argumentative fervour, and in some senses makes a greater
impact than the truth, the counter-assertion will carry more
conviction than the plain statement of an obvious, platitudinous
or predictable truth.

However, it is appropriate to recall the distinction which
Behler[3] draws in his book on *Klassische und Romantische*

---

[3] E. Behler, *Klassische und Romantische Ironie* (Darmstadt, Wissenschaftliche
Buchgesellschaft, 1972).

Ironie. Here he refers to a stable, or 'classical', irony where the
rhetorical device is manipulated to produce a stable 'counter-
reading' from the audience, and an unstable, or Romantic, irony
where no clear-cut meaning may be inferred. Much of the irony
of Grass's *Die Blechtrommel* belongs to this second category of
irony.

An additional element in the response to verbal irony is the
fact that, as Muecke maintains, there is a special pleasure in
interpreting it, 'in seeing in a set of words a meaning, moreover,
that contradicts the meaning that *is* there' (*15*, p.63). In short,
the reader is not invited to share the author's or narrator's statement of a particular truth, but he is forced to produce his own
version of the truth. The meaning exists not on the page of the
book, but in the countermanding response of the reader (if one
may be allowed a gross over-simplification). The ironic
statement raises at least three problems: firstly, the problem of
recognition, whether, in other words, the surface meaning is to
be accepted or rejected; secondly, if rejection is appropriate, to
what extent can the reader even feel sure that he has pieced
together the intended meaning, which, as one might expect, is
concealed; and thirdly, since the author does not reveal his
meaning directly, the reader's version of the truth will be open-
ended, and he will have difficulties in knowing where to set a
limit to the extent of the truth. A fourth problem arises with
irony and this is the converse of the problem of interpreting
irony: if an author is an habitual ironist, can one recognise a
serious, non-ironic statement with confidence and how much
importance does one attach to an ostensibly serious statement
which is embedded in a framework of irony? This is a question
to which we shall return later.

A good example of rhetorical irony occurs in the chapter
which describes Agnes Matzerath's death and funeral. Meyn and
Scheffler notice the presence of the Jewish toy dealer at the
funeral and forcibly escort him from the cemetery:

> Und beide gaben acht, daß der Markus, der rückwärts
> ging, nicht über Gräbereinfassungen stolperte, schoben ihn
> auf die Hauptallee und zeigten dem Sigismund, wo das

> Friedhofstor war. Der schien sich für die Auskunft zu bedanken und ging Richtung Ausgang, setzte sich auch den Zylinder auf und blickte sich nicht mehr um, obgleich Meyn und der Bäckermeister ihm nachblickten (p.134).

The obvious example of rhetorical irony consists in the use of the term 'sich bedanken', though the ground for this usage is prepared in advance by its not uncommon employment as an ironical expression in everyday speech. The idea that the bouncers are taking care to ensure that Markus does not lose his balance is equally ironical, though the reader himself does not need to contradict this, for the narrator performs this task for him by suggesting that Markus's companions are not taking him initially along a pathway, but pushing him over gravestones and furthermore that he is being propelled backwards. As usual the narrator is engaged in an act of double-stopping: he is expecting the reader to react to two notes at the same time. On the one hand the reader is amused by the scene, which can readily be appreciated in visual terms, and on the other hand he is shocked by the inhumanity of the Christians to the Jewish intruder. It is a non-stereotyped illustration of anti-Semitism and this serves to heighten its impact, for the author is not channelling the reader's feelings along a well-worn groove. This passage accords with Philip Thomson's definition of the grotesque as 'the unresolved clash of incompatibles in work and response' (*25*, p.27).

The section that follows also illustrates another problem which arises in an ironic work of art: the juxtaposition of the ironic and the non-ironic statements. Oskar detaches himself from the adult mourners and seeks out the company of his supplier of drums, much to the latter's amazement:

> 'Das Oskarchen!' wunderte sich der Markus, 'nu sag, was machen se middem Markus? Was hadder getan, dasse so tun?' Ich wußte nicht, was Markus getan hatte, nahm ihn bei seiner schweißnassen Hand, führte ihn durchs schmiedeeisern offenstehende Friedhofstor ... (p.134).

Markus's question is a non-ironic, incredulous expression of his inability to explain the reasons for the brutal behaviour to which he has been subjected. The second question is the fundamental question to which there is no reply in moral terms. It serves as a condemnation of the action of his persecutors. It is a simple, uncomplicated response of the innocent victim. The impact of these questions is heightened by the irony of the previous passage and a further intensification takes place when Oskar produces a remark — though not to Markus — in the manner of the naive, uncomprehending child. It is the response of a child, who in childlike manner thinks that all questions should be answered. In this sense it could be maintained that Oskar's statement is ironic because it is based upon pretence and in another sense it accords totally with the truth of the situation — it is ironical and truthful simultaneously. A further twist in the narrative thread, and a further claim on the reader's responsiveness, are provided by the appearance of Schugger Leo whose comically deranged behaviour is paralleled by the actions of Meyn and Scheffler and leaves the reader wondering whether any dividing line can be found between the two types of madness. Thus irony as a rhetorical device is embedded in a series of stylistic devices all of which make varying claims on the reader's susceptibilities, appealing to a range of feelings either at one and the same time or in quick succession. The passage as a whole has clearly pronounced satiric overtones.

Another example of irony as a rhetorical device occurs after Oskar has launched his voice against the windows of the town theatre and shattered the glass. He reports on his experiences in the following terms:

> Indem ich die Foyerfenster unseres Stadttheaters zersang, suchte und fand ich zum erstenmal Kontakt mit der Bühnenkunst. Mama muß trotz starker Beanspruchung durch den Spielzeughändler Markus an jenem Nachmittag mein direktes Verhältnis zum Theater bemerkt haben, denn während der folgenden Weihnachtszeit kaufte sie vier Theaterkarten, für sich, für Stephan und Marga Bronski, auch für Oskar, und nahm uns drei am letzten Advents-sonntag zum Weihnachtsmärchen mit (p.86).

As is often the case with irony the mode of expression is matter-of-fact, casual; it has the appearance of reasonableness and preserves an air of ostensible detachment. Yet Oskar's references to his contact with the theatrical arts and to his direct relationship with the theatre are clearly fantastic. The reader immediately disputes the correctness of these assertions. He does this with the knowledge that Oskar's only experience of the theatre has been his vocal assault on its window panes and shortly he will also discover that Oskar continues this tradition by rendering one of the theatre's spotlights ineffective. The reader is thus aware of the double meaning of these two statements, the superficial meaning and the implied meaning. If, however, the novel as a whole is reviewed, then Oskar's direct relationship with the theatre acquires a new dimension. It emerges throughout the course of the novel that Oskar revels in histrionics and that his delight in role-playing is nothing more than an extension of the pleasure he derives from dissembling. A prime example of his theatrical capabilities can be found in the final chapter of the book in which he feigns fear in order to justify his flight and give credibility to his madness. In connection with Oskar's direct relationship with the theatre one could legitimately speak of three levels of meaning: the narrator's apparent falsehood is negated by the reader who on more mature reflection may feel stimulated into revising his counter-assertion.

With these two examples of rhetorical irony, as with all the examples with which we have been dealing, the five basic features of irony to which Muecke refers in his book are clearly in evidence: 'a confident unawareness (real or pretended), a contrast of appearance and reality, a comic element, an element of detachment and an aesthetic element' (*15*, p.48) The first condition of irony is fulfilled by Oskar, the narrator and ingénu, who with a simulated yet confident unawareness produces all manner of assertions, ranging from falsehood to truth. The presence of an aesthetic element will by now also be apparent to the reader. The passages we have been examining have all been finely shaped and structured, the incongruities sharply focussed and juxtaposed, the narrator's detached air of unawareness highlighted, and the comic element finely tuned to produce the maximum desired effect. The casualness of Oskar's manner which is part of the detachment typical of irony must not divert the reader from the realisation that *Die Blechtrommel* is characterised by a high degree of artistry.

Northrop Frye[4] has maintained that satire is militant irony, and the close connection between satire and irony has not escaped our attention in the discussion of the preceding passages. Given the fact that satire is more aggressive than irony and that its objective is to expose to ridicule the stupidity of man, its detection usually presents fewer problems than irony, though the combination of two or more disparate elements is still the hallmark of satire as it is with irony. It responds to the world with a mixture of laughter and indignation: mirth accompanies moral purpose. Throughout the novel satire is to be encountered usually, as might be expected, in close proximity to irony and to the grotesque, and its appreciation is not facilitated by the presence of criteria which are intended to guide the judgement of the reader. True to its affinity with irony, the satire derives its impetus from the contrast of incongruities. Oskar in any case cannot provide any yardstick, for he is the naive, childlike observer who, like Simplicissimus in Grimmelshausen's novel, has supposedly no moral standards by which assessment would be possible. A fine example of satirical reduction is provided by Meyn's exclusion from the SA:

> Selbst als sich der SA-Mann während der Nacht vom achten zum neunten November achtunddreißig, die man später die Kristallnacht nannte, besonders mutig hervortat, die Langfuhrer Synagoge im Michaelisweg mit anderen in Brand steckte, auch kräftig mittat, als am folgenden Morgen mehrere, zuvor genau bezeichnete Geschäfte geräumt werden mußten, konnte all sein Eifer seine Entfernung aus der Reiter-SA nicht verhindern. Wegen unmenschlicher Tierquälerei wurde er degradiert und von der Mitgliederliste gestrichen (p.162).

[4] Northrop Frye, *The Anatomy of Criticism* (Princeton, Princeton U.P., 1957).

The satire in this context is based upon the fact that Meyn is dismissed from the SA not on account of his brutality to the Jews but on account of his cruelty to animals. This is the fundamental discrepancy, which is, however, delicately manipulated in order to give edge to the incisiveness. The description of Meyn's behaviour is placed in the mouth of Oskar who plays the naive, uncomprehending child, can pretend to present Meyn's actions on the night of the *Kristallnacht* as an act of bravery and furthermore can maintain that the attack was launched not against individuals — and in any case the word Jew is never mentioned — but against property. Oskar adds credibility to his claims by mentioning specific details, for example, the date of the incident and the name of the synagogue, thus anchoring an extravagant statement in the context of a realistic, historically defined world. The factual references enhance the air of objectivity, which Oskar, the ostensibly detached observer, is at pains to preserve. The contrast between the appearance, which the narrator depicts and which he would have us believe, and the reality, of which the reader has in any case some knowledge, is horrifying. The understatement which is contained in the reference to the evacuation rather than the ransacking of the shops or the imprisonment or murder of their owners is yet another example of the fine tuning of the passage and its pronounced aesthetic effect. Oskar, the ingenuous narrator, does not confront reality but approaches it obliquely, thus producing a travesty of the situation. The narrator's naivety is not his alone, it interlocks with the naivety (and callousness) of a world in which people are fired for cruelty to animals and promoted for the slaughter of humans. The comic and the critical effect stems from the clash between appearance and reality and is heightened by the child-like naivety of the observer and the aesthetic fashioning of the passage concerned.

The target of the satirical irony in *Die Blechtrommel* tends to be mainly but not exclusively political, but since, to judge by Matthew Hodgart,[5] the two principal topics of satire are politics and women, this is hardly surprising. National Socialism, as we

[5] Matthew Hodgart, *Satire* (London, Weidenfeld and Nicolson, 1969).

have seen in the previous quotation, is obviously a subject which is frequently exposed to attack. Another such example is provided in the chapter which describes Herbert Truczinski's fateful encounter with the galleon figurehead named Niobe. The latter is suspected of having caused the death of a number of men, and her case provokes a good deal of discussion:

> Man diskutierte hin und her, richtete in den Zeitungen eigens für den Fall Niobe eine Ecke für freie Meinungs-äußerung ein; von fatalen Begebenheiten wurde gesprochen (p.153).

The year is 1938, as our narrator indicates at the beginning of the chapter (p.147). Thus this piece of ironic foolery derides by implication the lack of freedom in the Danzig press. However, a second level of irony emerges when this statement is placed against the background of the chapter as a whole and the subsequent chapter which has as its focal point the *Kristallnacht* and Meyn's participation in the persecution of the Jews. The case of Niobe acquires in the narrative context of the novel political overtones of which the Nazis are ironically unaware. Niobe becomes emblematic of the misfortune which controls the destiny of the people and which, either at the time or retrospectively, the Germans regard as the origins of their misery. She is the source of all 'Unglück' (see p.151) in the same way that the economic miracle is the source of all 'Glück' in the post-war period (see pp.367-68). She is indicative of the forces which deprive men of their will to resist, is a portent of future ill-starred fortune, and she becomes the means of lampooning the fatalistic surrender of the Germans to the forces of unreason. Thus at the beginning of the next chapter entitled 'Glaube Hoffnung Liebe' we read the following:

> Das Weib starb nicht. Das wurde versiegelt und im Museumskeller, angeblich wegen Restaurationsarbeiten, aufbewahrt. Doch man kann das Unglück nicht einkellern. Mit den Abwässern findet es durch die Kanalisation, es teilt sich den Gasleitungen mit, kommt allen Haus-

haltungen zu, und niemand, der da sein Suppentöpfchen
auf die bläulichen Flammen stellt, ahnt, daß da das
Unglück seinen Fraß zum Kochen bringt (p.159).

Thus the first quotation referring to Niobe may be described as
an example of double-layered ironic satire. The primary
meaning proceeds from the reader's response to Oskar's ironic
utterance and can be appreciated within the context of the one
sentence, providing, of course, that the reader has some
knowledge of the political circumstances operating at the time.
The secondary meaning is only apparent once the reader has
placed it against the background of the chapter to which it
belongs and the following chapter. The link with the post-war
period is evident only at a much later stage in the novel. The
complex interconnections which derive from a network of
associations spanning the great divide of 1945 destroy any fond
illusion which the reader may harbour in thinking that *Die
Blechtrommel* is merely a series of loosely connected stories. The
last quotation does draw our attention to a problem to which all
commentators on irony refer, namely the difficulty which the
reader may experience in determining whether a statement of a
narrator is intentionally or unconsciously ironical. In many
works of art the problem could easily be disregarded because it
cannot readily be resolved and/or its resolution is of no
particular account. In *Die Blechtrommel* the issue is of more
substantial importance in that it could assist the reader in
deciding whether Oskar is merely a narrative device and hence
by virtue of his office, cannot accept any guilt, or whether he is a
character in his own right and hence subject to a moral code.

The glorious virtues of war are also unceremoniously knocked
off their pedestal. Fritz Truczinski's activities as a member of
the German Air Force are reduced in stature by the following
understatement, which is inserted in a list of Western capitals:
'der Kerl war immer auf Dienstreisen' (p.221). His death is
stripped of every heroic quality: 'Der Unteroffizier Fritz
Truczinski war für drei Dinge gleichzeitig gefallen: für Führer,
Volk und Vaterland' (p.291). Both quotations are typical
examples of the basic technique of satire in that they belittle or

devalue attitudes of mind. The individual or the attitude he represents is reduced in stature and in dignity. Equally well the alliterative reference to 'Führer, Volk und Vaterland' as three things in addition to the incongruous inclusion of the word 'gleichzeitig' introduces a comic element and suggests also the futility of his death whilst possibly implying that his sacrifice was scarcely heeded by the German war machine. As usual we are confronted with an irony which makes its appeal to a number of emotions at the same time and is open-ended in its range of possible interpretations. As we have noted elsewhere the criteria by which the ironic voice may be recognised are not indicated in the statements that are made. The reader has to rely on himself and must be ready to detect the appropriate warning signals, foremost amongst which is the disparity between appearance and reality coupled with the comic element. He must penetrate behind the mask of the dissembler.

The post-war period with its inability to come to terms with the past and with its rampant materialism is not spared the satiric onslaught. Here again an absence of a yardstick which would supply the reader with a sense of orientation is a feature of the ironic presentation. The chapter entitled 'Die letzte Straßenbahn oder Anbetung eines Weckglases' illustrates this point. In this chapter two officials who are relics from the Nazi period attempt in the year 1951 to arrest and execute one of the few survivors of the defence of the Polish Post Office, and the two henchmen are presented as being worthy of sympathy because of the inconvenience which fulfilling their duty imposes upon them:

Seine ganze Freizeit, auch die Ferien müsse er opfern, damit ein Erschießungsbefehl aus dem Jahre neunund-dreißig endlich ausgeführt werde, schließlich habe er noch einen Beruf, sei Handelsvertreter, und sein Kumpel habe als Ostflüchtling gleichfalls seine Schwierigkeiten, der müsse noch mal ganz von vorne anfangen, habe im Osten eine gutgehende Maßschneiderei verloren, aber jetzt sei Feierabend; heute nacht wird der Befehl ausgeführt, dann ist Schluß mit der Vergangenheit — wie gut, daß wir noch die Straßenbahn erwischt haben (p.478).

The aggressiveness of satire, in this case the monstrousness of executing a defender of the Polish Post Office in accordance with a Nazi directive of 1939, makes it readily recognisable as a mode of expression. Equally, the clear-cut nature of the onslaught facilitates the reader's application of moral criteria. The satire in this instance is based upon a double ironic structure: the ostensibly naive narrator, Oskar, presents us in consciously ironic manner with the statement of an individual who unconsciously ironises himself by exposing to ridicule the absurd and inhuman nature of his attitude and behaviour. The unemotional matter-of-factness of the details which the official supplies creates the air of detachment which, as we have noted elsewhere, is one of the characteristics of irony. As usual we are confronted with the combination of the amusing and the serious, with the comic and the tragic.

The coexistence of amusement and disgust, of laughter and horror, mirth and revulsion which is often a feature of the satire one encounters in *Die Blechtrommel* has much in common with the grotesque. Kurt Lothar Tank has drawn our attention to the fact that Grass's liking for the grotesque is evident on almost every page of his works: 'Grass bedient sich der klassischen Groteske, weil darin, wie er sagt, "alles, das Tragische und das Komische und das Satirische, nebeneinander Raum hat, sich gegenseitig stützt"': Oskar Matzerath bleibe eine realistische Figur, werde nicht zum Kunstgeschöpf. Im Gegensatz zu der zuweilen unergiebigen, oft nur mechanisch funktionierenden Groteske in den Dramen (*Zweiunddreißig Zähne*, *Die bösen Köche*) gelang es Grass in der *Blechtrommel*, die Möglichkeiten der klassischen Groteske auszunutzen' (*23*, p.61).

The grotesque, it could be claimed, is one of the means, perhaps the best means, of coming to terms with a reality as sordid and brutal as that of National Socialism, in accordance with Dürrenmatt's principle that in our present world the assumptions of tragedy appear ridiculous and that we can cope with our epoch only through the medium of comedy. In his book on the grotesque Wolfgang Kayser[6] has expressed the same basic

[6] Wolfgang Kayser, *The Grotesque in Art and Literature*, trans. Ulrich Weisstein (Bloomington, Indiana U.P., 1963), p.188.

idea by stating that 'the grotesque is an attempt to invoke and subdue the demonic aspects of the world'. Philip Thomson refers to this process in slightly different terms: 'the grotesque does serve to bring the horrifying and disgusting aspects of existence to the surface, there to be rendered less harmful by the introduction of a comic perspective' (*25*, p.59). In this sense the grotesque achieves a liberating effect comparable to the cathartic effect which tragedy is supposed to produce, a type of abreaction which allows the release of repressed emotion. However, true to the duality, if not ambivalence, of the response it calls forth, the grotesque achieves not only a liberating effect but also creates tension and anxiety.

Oskar's description of the death of Roswitha Raguna may be regarded as a good example of the grotesque:

> Da sprang sie selbst vom Wagen, lief mit dem Koch-geschirr in Stöckelschuhen auf die Feldküche zu und erreichte den heißen Morgenkaffee gleichzeitig mit einer dort einschlagenden Schiffsgranate (p.285).

In a well-nigh literal sense such a situation corresponds to Philip Thomson's already quoted definition of the grotesque as 'the unresolved clash of incompatibles in work and response' (see *25*). The combination of laughter and horror recalls the fact that both Oskar and Klepp react to situations in a manner which is similar to the reader's response to this set of circumstances. On one occasion Oskar describes Klepp as an individual:

> dem schließlich jede, noch so peinliche menschliche Situation wie ein vortrefflicher Spaß schmeckte ... (p.443).

Laughter and horror can be so intermingled, so inseparable, that the reader can appreciate Oskar's exaggeration when he claims that for Klepp the concepts of weeping and laughter are completely unclear (see p.441). Oskar also comments upon the way he is affected by sentimental films involving nurses:

> Während Oskars Kleinhirn und Großhirn lachten und

Unanständigkeiten am laufenden Band dem Filmstreifen
einflochten, weinten Oskars Augen Tränen, ich irrte
halbblind in einer Wüste ... (p.401).

Oskar's statement here reminds the reader of Walpole's
observation that the world is a comedy to those who think and a
tragedy to those who feel. In *Die Blechtrommel* the reader is
called upon to react, like Oskar, simultaneously in rational and
emotional terms, in such a way, however, that the two or more
elements within the reader's response conflict one with another.

Another death — that of Albrecht Greff, the greengrocer —
provides a further example of the grotesque. Greff, who has just
received a summons to appear in court because of a sexual
offence, hangs himself in the cellar of his shop so that when his
body is released, a weird set of sounds is produced:

Während unten die Kartoffeln übers und vom Podest auf
den Betonboden polterten, schlug es oben auf Blech, Holz,
Bronze, Glas, hämmerte oben ein entfesseltes Trommel-
orchester Albrecht Greffs großes Finale (p.260).

The comic element which is a recurring feature of the grotesque
is indeed present in this instance. However, the comic is
outweighed by the fearful, if not gruesome, element. The
detachment with which this scene is described produces an
alienating and disorientating effect upon the mind of the reader.
So nonplussed is he that any didactic point that may be present
tends to be obscured, and this is so even if the reader draws the
parallel between Greff's personal predicament and the
impending disaster of the German army in Stalingrad towards
the end of 1942. Unlike satire the grotesque does not provide a
scale of values which allows a clear-cut differentiation between
right and wrong, nor are there even any implied criteria. It may
even be claimed that not only are the comic and the horrific
inextricably intermingled, but that right and wrong are also
absurdly inseparable. The reader suffers from this same sense of
bewilderment in encountering and assessing Schugger Leo whose
insane behaviour and utterances are yet again instances of the

grotesque.

The description of the fear which grips Jan Bronski in the closing stages of the defence of the Polish Post Office is yet another instance of the 'unresolved clash of incompatibles in work and response' and also illustrates how extravagance and excess are often hallmarks of the grotesque:

> Angst besetzte ihn von unten nach oben, flutete von oben nach unten zurück, fand unten, vielleicht wegen der Schuhsohlen mit Einlagen, so starken Widerstand, daß die Angst sich Luft machen wollte, aber zurückprallte, über Magen, Milz und Leber flüchtend in seinem armen Kopf dergestalt Platz nahm, daß ihm die Blauaugen vorquollen und verzwickte Äderchen im Weiß zeigten, die Oskar am Augapfel seines mutmaßlichen Vaters wahrzunehmen, zuvor nicht Gelegenheit gefunden hatte (pp.186-87).

The surging ebb and flow of Bronski's fear achieves an amusing effect and, fantastic though the idea is in purely anatomical terms, it serves equally to conjure up his acute sense of terror and it could be claimed that the terrifying element is thereby heightened. Furthermore — and this may also be regarded as a typical feature of the grotesque — the imaginative extravagance is not divorced from reality, for the fantastic operates within the framework of the real, and in a perverse, paradoxical manner the two elements, just as much as the comic and the tragic, support and accentuate each other. The disharmony between the fanciful and the real, the comic and the terrifying, is a source of stimulation, creates a unique aesthetic sensation, provides a new perspective and breaks down hitherto accepted modes of feeling and thinking. Bronski is gripped by fear in a world which is our world, and the grotesque, with its conscious or unconscious confusion of the fanciful and the real, serves as a means of expressing the inexplicable.

A further example of the grotesque in which the fantastic and the real complement and conflict with one another can be found in the chapter 'Glaube Hoffnung Liebe' in which an SA man in grim saturnalian manner approaches Sigismund Markus only to find that the Jew has committed suicide:

> Einer, der Kasperlepuppen an den Fingern hatte, stieß ihn
> mit Kasperles Großmutter hölzern an, aber Markus war
> nicht mehr zu sprechen, nicht mehr zu kränken. Vor ihm
> auf der Schreibtischplatte stand ein Wasserglas, das
> auszuleeren ihm ein Durst gerade in jenem Augenblick
> geboten haben mußte, als die splitternd aufschreiende
> Schaufensterscheibe seines Ladens seinen Gaumen trocken
> werden ließ (p.164).

As usual the comic and the horrifying form an inseparable
mixture both in terms of their coexistence in the passage itself
and in the reader's response, though it could be claimed that the
terrifying, repulsive element is in the ascendancy. Horrific
though this situation is, the comic constitutes almost a kind of
safety-valve, even if its presence tends to highlight and heighten
the gruesome quality.

Thus, as we have established in the course of this discussion,
irony is the basic principle within the novel simply because the
narrator revels in dissimulation. However, the irony of which
dissembling and double meaning are characteristic features may
shift, almost imperceptibly, into related modes of expression
such as satire and the grotesque. In the battle of identification it
may be well to recall that all three modes depend upon the
incongruity of conflicting elements, that satire is militant irony
where the criteria are stated or clearly implied, whilst the
grotesque dispenses with the moral yardstick and indignation,
and hence may lack the didactic thrust associated with satire.
Furthermore it has been maintained that 'irony is primarily
intellectual in its function and appeal, and the grotesque
primarily emotional' (*25*, p.47).

One final question may be posed: amidst the welter of irony,
satire and the grotesque, what chance does the serious statement, which is neither overstatement nor understatement, have
of being recognised and appreciated as such? It would seem that,
in the same way that the comic enhances the impact of the tragic
in that double embrace called the grotesque, the serious state-

ment embedded in the framework of irony also acquires additional poignancy. An excellent example of such a statement occurs during the attack on the Polish Post Office during the course of which Jan Bronski is goaded by Kobyella into firing off his rifle (the observation in question is very similar to one made by Kafka to Janouch):

> Mein mutmaßlicher Vater hatte eine solch genaue und bei all seiner weich üppigen Phantasie realistische Vorstellung vom Krieg, daß es ihm schwer fiel, ja, unmöglich war, aus mangelnder Einbildungskraft mutig zu sein (p.187).

The screw of poignancy is tightened still further when Jan Bronski, in retreat from reality, bids the dying Kobyella to join in a game of *Skat*, though in this instance the reader is once again in the realm of the grotesque with the absurd reinforcing the impact of the emotional element. The same quality of pathos is evoked when Fajngold, after inspecting Matzerath's corpse, ushers his family into the cellar:

> Seine ganze Familie, nicht nur die Frau Luba, rief er in den Keller, und sicherlich sah er alle kommen, denn er nannte sie beim Namen, sagte Luba, Lew, Jakub, Berek, Leon, Mendel und Zonja, erklärte den Genannten, wer da liege und tot sei und erklärte gleich darauf uns, daß alle, die er soeben gerufen habe, auch so dalagen, bevor sie in die Öfen von Treblinka kamen, dazu noch seine Schwägerin und der Schwägerin Schwestermann, der fünf Kinderchen hatte, und alle lagen, nur er, der Herr Fajngold, lag nicht, weil er Chlor streuen mußte (p.329).

What appears initially as a serious statement quickly emerges as an ambivalent statement in which the comic element — the idea that Fajngold introduces the members of his family and speaks to them — is overshadowed by the horror and the pity which the reader experiences in the face of the absurdity and futility of their death. The feeling which is aroused in favour of the Jew and his family is given further impetus by the fact that Fajngold is presented, or presents himself, as a person whose mind has been partially or totally unhinged by his suffering. The statement is 'serious' only in the sense that the comic has a severely reduced impact and the direction of the emotional appeal is unambiguous and clear-cut. In this instance, encouraging the reader to feel for a character diminishes the impression of absurdity, if absurd is defined as 'out of harmony with reason or propriety.'[7] The reader is in effect called upon to react against the absurdity of the Jewish plight, and in this sense the oblique recourse to moral indignation is a revolt against the apparent futility and purposelessness of their fate. It is important to recall that the 'consistent perception of the grotesque, or the perception of grotesqueness on a grand scale, can lead to the notion of universal absurdity' (*25*, p.32). The shaping of the emotional response, enlisting the sympathy of the reader, will tend to counter this danger, as will the inclusion of satire with its implied, relatively unambiguous criteria. However, the conventionally serious statement which is to be understood at its face value is a rare occurrence in *Die Blechtrommel*. Admittedly, this is hardly unexpected in a work of art which has an ironic narrative viewpoint, in which satire and especially the grotesque abound, and in which psychological analysis is supplanted by caricature.

[7] *Shorter Oxford Dictionary*, 1965.

4. Narrative Skill

What attracts us to the novel in the first instance is the author's highly developed capacity for story-telling which supplies the novel with its momentum. From the first chapter onwards we are fascinated by the series of episodes which are connected directly or indirectly with the central figure of the novel. The first chapter sets the tone: Oskar's grandfather, Joseph Koljaiczek, is attempting to escape from the clutches of the German police and takes refuge from his pursuers under the voluminous Kashubian skirts of Anna Bronski, who is conveniently sitting by the side of a fire in a potato field. Having entered the sanctuary formed by Anna's four skirts, he puts his time to good use by founding a dynasty. Within hours the two of them are united in marriage. The episode is not untypical: the narrative concentrates upon the actions and the observable behaviour of the characters concerned. There is no sense in which the author concerns himself with the inward world of man. Rather does the converse seem to be true: feelings and thoughts are objectivised, i.e. they are reflected in the objects and situations which comprise the external world. Rarely does the tension created by the story-telling slacken. Sometimes the unusual perspective of the narrative adds a special flavour to the episodes. The absurd and the grotesque both heighten the narrative élan. And it must be admitted that a pinch of blasphemy or obscenity adds spice to Grass's literary recipe. Oskar's amorous adventures are especially intriguing and grip the reader's attention whilst at the same time being rich in comic effect. A number of these stand out in the reader's mind: Oskar's and Maria's adolescent love for each other erupts with volcanic fury under the influence of sherbet; in order to escape Maria's insidious spell Oskar falls victim to Frau Greff whose stench bludgeons our hero's senses into submission — we learn how he joins her in bed fully clothed with his shoes on and

appreciates the washing facilities which the husband supplies
after the operations have been completed; another amorous
interlude is provided by Oskar's gymnastics on the coconut
matting which, placed between him and the lady of his choice,
constitutes an effective but rather itchy form of insulation. Such
episodes — and probably the majority in the novel — can be
enjoyed for their own sake without reference to previous events.
Nor is there any need to occupy oneself with the background
political happenings or to be aware of the significance, or even
presence, of the imagery. One can be entertained by the anec-
dotes without being unduly troubled by Oskar's unreliability as
a narrator, such is the gusto with which such stories are told.
One enters into Oskar's world of fantasy and is delighted by the
imaginative inventiveness which gives shape to the series of
incidents within the narrative. In this way we frequently find
that our disbelief is suspended and our doubt made to look
superfluous. Henri Plard[8] has summarised Günter Grass's skill
as a story-teller in the following terms: 'Ich wüßte keinen von
den jüngeren deutschen Erzählern zu nennen, der so unmittelbar
und primitiv packend wie Günter Grass zu berichten wüßte.
Gemeint ist hier die einfache Kunst, den Leser in Atem zu halten
wie bei einem Krimi von Klasse' (p.48).

In describing how he came to write *Die Blechtrommel*, Grass
refers to his obsession with detail (*8*, p.18) and constantly
throughout the novel we encounter examples of his meticulous
preoccupation with detail, as though he wanted to gather into
his novel the multi-faceted range of all created things. One is not
surprised to read Grass's remark: 'Sprache hatte mich als
Durchfall erwischt' (*8*, p.15). His insistence on precision in the
description of Oskar's external world manifests itself in a
number of ways. The actions and events in each episode are
recounted in a systematic manner, even if the content stems
from the realm of fantasy, whether this be the history of Niobe,
the drumming machine on which Greff commits suicide, the
unearthing of a corpse (in the chapter entitled 'Fortuna Nord')
or Oskar's antics on the coconut matting. On other occasions
Grass's obsession with detail is evident in the location of the

[8] Henri Plard, 'Über *Die Blechtrommel*' in *1*.

action in a quite specific environment and this may take the form of listing facts or pseudo-facts. The description of Danzig as an inferno following air raids and artillery attack is a case in point:

> Es brannten die Häkergasse, Langgasse, Breitgasse, Große und Kleine Wollwebergasse, es brannten die Tobiasgasse, Hundegasse, der Altstädtische Graben, Vorstädtische Graben, die Wälle brannten und die Lange Brücke. Das Krantor war aus Holz und brannte besonders schön. In der Kleinen Hosennähergasse ließ sich das Feuer für mehrere auffallend grelle Hosen Maß nehmen. Die Marienkirche brannte von innen nach außen und zeigte Festbeleuchtung durch Spitzbogenfenster (p.322).

In the final pages of the book the reader is presented with a series of reminiscences which take the form of objects and events with which Oskar has been associated. The narrator conjures up the past by collecting and recollecting the things which have been for him nodes of experience. In both these examples, the burning down of Danzig and Oskar's review of his life, the reader is aware of the author's delight in sensuous detail. Such cataloguing serves the remembrance of things past and it is as though the readers were exposed to the onslaught of life itself in all its visual immediacy. Sometimes a single word is sufficient to unleash a torrent of associated words and correspondences, as is the case when Oskar prods the word 'cross' into feverish activity (pp.112-13). The phrase 'Der Falter trommelte' provokes Oskar on another occasion into engaging in linguistic acrobatics, whilst at the same time giving added substance and significance to what appears at first sight to be quite a simple sentence (p.36). The totality of the external world in all its varied manifestations, or so it would seem, assails our senses. Grass's universal embrace anchors us to *terra firma* and rescues us from the dark abyss of romance into which Oskar's fantasy and untrustworthiness would plunge us. Moreover, one could also regard the attention to physical detail as a function of the child's perspective. The reader may well recall Grass's observations about Döblin, his

literary mentor: 'Der Gegenstand des Romans ist die entfesselte
Realität ... Im Roman heißt es schichten, häufen, wälzen,
schieben; im Drama, dem jetzigen, auf die Handlung hin
verarmten, handlungsverbohrten: "voran!" Vorwärts ist
niemals die Parole des Romans' (*9*, p.11). In *Die Blechtrommel*
Grass certainly unleashes the reality of the external world upon
the reader who is then subjected to wave upon wave of attack.
Paradoxically, this reality constitutes, in all its complexity, a
stabilising factor within the novel.

5. Imagery

Imagery also contributes to the coherence of *Die Blechtrommel* as a whole, though much of it is not accessible to the reader when he approaches the novel for the first time. In examining the imagery in *Die Blechtrommel* — and for that matter in other narrative works of Grass — it is appropriate to recall that Grass, in an interview with Heinz Ludwig Arnold, has said that poetry is the art form which suits him most and that he started his literary career as a lyricist (*1*, p.17). Hence one may expect that poetic usage will be of significance in Grass's works. It is obvious, even from a superficial reading of the novel, that certain words occur frequently within the text, reinforcing already existent associations and gathering fresh ones in the process. They constitute nodes of experience and present 'an intellectual and emotional complex in an instant of time'.[9] The images are allowed to stand alone, 'teasing our understanding by nondiscursive relationship with what surrounds them.'[10] In that Grass provides no theoretical explanation of their meaning, they force the reader to come to his own conclusions. As has been stated elsewhere, Grass presents us with a series of stories which have a partial independence of their own and can be enjoyed in their own right. Nevertheless the concrete particulars and the arrangement of the stories carry meanings beyond immediate significance. As with Joyce's *Ulysses*, imagery and juxtaposition, both devices which are more frequently encountered in poetry, supplement the narrative. Imagery may even form the starting-point from which the episode develops. It is not coincidental that many of the titles of the chapters refer, not to people or actions, but to objects, e.g. 'Der weite Rock', 'Unterm Floß', 'Falter und Glühbirne', 'Die Tribüne', 'Das Kartenhaus',

[9] Ezra Pound as quoted in *26*, p.187.

[10] William York Tindall, *The Literary Symbol* (Bloomington and London, Indiana U. P., 1955), p.117.

'Brausepulver', 'Die Ameisenstraße', 'Der Ringfinger' etc. In an interview with Burton Pike,[11] Grass has stated that he is not interested in psychological characterisation, but rather in presenting a character surrounded by the objects of his milieu. 'The characters', so he maintains, 'don't explain themselves by means of the inner monologue or lectures about their tensions, but through quite simple relationships: what they do with food and furniture for instance'. It is true that the objects with which Grass surrounds his characters and which take on the role of Eliot's 'objective correlative' are allusive and not always totally explicable. Nevertheless, the strange paradox arises in *Die Blechtrommel*, that, though the narrator is untrustworthy and engenders an atmosphere of doubt, the objects, their associations and their correspondences sometimes, though not necessarily, speak a clearer language and may unmask the ironic narrator. Wayne C. Booth has commented upon the function of imagery in the modern novel: 'with commentary ruled out, hundreds of devices remain for revealing judgement and moulding responses. Patterns of imagery and symbol are as effective in modern fiction as they have always been in poetry in controlling our evaluation of details' (*2*, p.272). The accumulation of associations knits the narrative together and as Jochen Rohlfs[12] has stated with regard to the chapter entitled 'Glaube Hoffnung Liebe' (p.238), 'Die Vergangenheit fließt in die Gegenwart der "Ich weiß nicht"-Kette ein, die Begriffe verlieren ihre klar umrissene Bedeutung, an Stelle unmittelbarer sprachlicher Logik tritt die Logik des assoziierenden Bewußtseins'. There are underlying trails of associations throughout the novel and Grass is frequently at pains to make evident the links between objects which perform a similar evocative function.

As is the case with *Katz und Maus* and *Hundejahre* the title of the book, and the dust-cover, force the central image or symbol into the forefront of the reader's consciousness from the outset.

[11] Burton Pike, 'Objects vs People in the recent German Novel', in *Wisconsin Studies in Contemporary Literature*, Autumn 1966, Vol.VII, No.3, p.307.

[12] Jochen Rohlfs, 'Erzählen aus unzuverlässiger Sicht. Zur Erzählstruktur bei Günter Grass', in *1*, p.57.

Grass observes the same convention with this title as he does with the titles of the individual chapters: the novel is called 'Die Blechtrommel' and not 'Der Blechtrommler', even though the poem which Grass wrote as a kind of experiment in narrative perspective was called 'Der Säulenheilige', and even though the dust-cover shows the drummer along with the drum. A number of associations which are attached to the drum and the drummer are apparent on the cover of the book: we see the grotesque figure of a boy with drum-sticks raised, presumably about to strike the drum; his body is strangely extended to form the background for the drum; the hat he wears is the kind a child might wear at a party or perhaps during carnival; the drummer is drawn in black and white apart from his eyes which are a bright blue; the drum is coloured red and white. When we come to read the novel, we find that the suggestiveness of the various colours is extended and reinforced: black is a sign of mourning and of evil, it has a menacing quality; blue recalls the fact that the typical German during the Nazi period was supposed to be blue-eyed and blond-haired, it is the favourite colour of the Romantics and is suggestive of spiritual intoxication; red and white are the national colours of Poland, whilst red in isolation is reminiscent of blood, transgression, rebelliousness, and white is traditionally the colour of innocence. There is a symbolism of colour within the novel, reminiscent perhaps of the way that Catholicism attaches specific meanings to various colours, though it would be wrong to think that each colour when it occurs in the text has an inevitable symbolic significance. The world Grass depicts in his novel is not transparent with meaning: the objects of sensory perception have their own colours and cannot be forced into a symbolic or allegorical pattern. The drum has at least two associations, even before we start reading the book: it is emblematic of war, for it can produce the rhythm which, as Oskar says, all men had to obey in 1914 (p.29), and yet it also conjures up the atmosphere of lamentation and of mourning. At the funeral of his mother, for instance, Oskar wants to express his grief by drumming on her coffin. And in Schlöndorff's film Oskar intones a doleful rhythm on his drum which takes on almost the quality of a funeral march. The

student of history will recall that Hitler was proud to be referred
to as a drummer and regarded this activity as his highest
aspiration,[13] though no link of this kind is established between
Hitler and Oskar in the novel. In *Die Blechtrommel* (and
presumably the advantage of the word 'Blech' is that is has two
meanings, i.e. 'tin' and 'rubbish' or 'nonsense') Oskar
Matzerath makes use of the drum as a means by which he can
preserve his status as a three-year-old. This central function of
the drum is one which Oskar emphasises on a number of
occasions; on this point the reader is left in no doubt as to how
the drum should be regarded. When, for example, Matzerath
wants to question his son about the robberies that have been
taking place in the jeweller's shop, Oskar refuses to give any
information:

> und versteckte mich mit immer größerem Geschick hinter
> meiner Blechtrommel und der permanenten Größe des
> zurückgebliebenen Dreijährigen (p.104).

In this way Oskar can erect a barrier between himself and the
adults who surround him, prevent their intrusion into his own
world of childish fantasy and can thereby evade any
responsibility. The drum allows Oskar to indulge in pretence
which is the precondition for his viewing the outside world in
ironic and grotesque terms. By means of the drum he can beat
the retreat from reality and avoid having to follow in his father's
footsteps as a shopkeeper: he can turn to art rather than to
business, and thus he parodies the dilemma with which many of
Thomas Mann's characters are confronted. He is a grotesque
distortion of Adrian Leverkühn, the musician who enters into a
pact with the devil and whose life is compared obliquely with
Germany's headlong plunge into destruction. The drum
epitomises Oskar's fundamental attitude of withdrawal from the
world of reality and is employed at the same time, as we have
indicated earlier in this study, as a narrative device by means of
which a period of history may be surveyed. The drum can also

[13] See Alan Bullock, *Hitler: A Study in Tyranny* (London, Odhams Press,
1952), p.117.

impinge on social reality as is evidenced in the effect Oskar achieves by playing on his drum at the Party rally.

Oskar would have us believe that the drum is his mode of expression, and that it is as it were part of his flesh and blood as he himself suggests (see p.176); the picture on the front of the book almost creates the impression that the drum is part of Oskar's body. The drum is hence Oskar's constant companion and, apart from a brief respite during the post-war period, it witnesses all the major events of his life, for the two of them are virtually inseparable. He even describes it on one occasion as the witness of his shame (p.211). Accordingly the drum is indicative of an attitude of mind. It also serves as a narrative device and draws the strands of the narrative together: in this sense it fulfils a recapitulatory function. Oskar introduces us to the drum in the second chapter of the novel; his mother promises him a drum for his third birthday (p.35); he develops his glass-shattering voice as a means of protecting his drum (in 'Glas, Glas, Gläschen'); the drum accompanies him on his one and only day at school; it helps him to break up a Party rally (in 'Die Tribüne'); he hangs it round the neck of Jesus hoping that the Saviour will produce a miracle of drumming (in 'Kein Wunder'); and he loses his supplier of drums when Sigismund Markus commits suicide during the course of the *Kristallnacht*. All these are events in the first book of the novel. The other two books of the novel are equally well provided with references to the drum and its associations. This symbol acquires a multi-faceted, allusive quality which constantly provokes the reader into discovering new and stimulating relationships between the various objects, characters and episodes in the novel. The reader comes to realise, as has been pointed out by Manfred Jurgensen, that the metaphorical language of Grass's literary works possesses 'einen argumentativen Grundzug' (*11a*, p.6). At the same time a symbol such as the drum — or for that matter the cat and mouse in Grass's 'Novelle' or the dog in *Hundejahre* — achieves a cohesive effect within the novel, and in conjunction with Grass's narrative skill acts as a counterweight to the ambivalence and ambiguity which are a characteristic of Oskar's narrative perspective. Oskar speaks the language of doubt; the metaphorical language, despite Oskar and as it were unbeknown to Oskar, sometimes reveals more than the narrator himself.

The imagery of 'Kopf' and 'Schwanz' is another example of metaphorical language which assumes an argumentative quality. This imagery and its related words occur sufficiently frequently for the reader to be tempted to think of them in terms of symbolism. René Wellek and Austin Warren remind us that 'an "image" may be invoked once as a metaphor, but if it persistently recurs, both as presentation and representation, it becomes a symbol, may even become part of a symbolic (or mythic) system' (*26*, p.189). The recurrent images in *Die Blechtrommel* operate, however, more in the no man's land which exists between imagery and symbolism in that, though they form nodes of hints and allusions, they may only seldom be considered fully fledged symbols: in other words, they rarely reach the stage of actually standing for or representing something quite specific. The words 'Kopf' and 'Schwanz' certainly come close to assuming the function of symbols in that, through the extension of already existent associations, the word 'Kopf' is developed as an allusive pointer to the values of reason and moderation which have been undermined by lustful passion and physical and political intoxication, as represented by the word 'Schwanz' with its sexual suggestiveness. Such imagery with its Nietzschean overtones occurs with particular force in the chapter entitled 'Karfreitagskost'. In this chapter Oskar describes how the sexual triangle of Agnes, Matzerath and Jan Bronski observe eels — by implication the equivalent of 'Schwanz' — devouring a horse's head. Agnes is nauseated by what she sees, for she regards it instinctively as the objectivisation of the passionate love affair in which she has been engaged with Jan Bronski. So sickened is she by the sight of the eels that she seeks escape from her adulterous relationship by poisoning herself with fish — yet another sexual image. In the same chapter Oskar retreats into his parents' wardrobe and in a dream visualises the sanctification of an eel, as part of what appears to be a grotesque communion service. He imagines seagulls settling on the sacrifice, an eel, and throwing it to Sister Inge, a nurse:

die fing ihn auch, feierte ihn und wurde zur Möwe, nahm
Gestalt an, nicht Taube, wenn schon heiliger Geist, dann in
jener Gestalt, die da Möwe heißt, sich als Wolke aufs
Fleisch senkt und Pfingsten feiert (p.128).

The picture of the eels eating the horse's head can be viewed as
the re-enactment of Agnes's personal predicament. As David
Roberts[14] observes, it can be regarded as an example of 'the
grotesque vision of life as the eternal cycle of the flesh that feeds
and is fed upon'. At the same time the imagery of head and tail
adumbrates the triumph of passion and lust over reason and
moderation which has implications on the personal and on the
political level. The same confrontation between reason and
unreason can be found in the juxtaposition of Goethe and
Rasputin on whom, so Oskar would have us believe, his
education is based. However, it is plain, in the chapter concerned, 'Rasputin und das ABC', where Goethe does not even
figure in the title, that lust, the 'Schwanz'-like principle of
Rasputin, emerges victorious over Goethe. This is evident in
equal measure elsewhere in the book, for example in the effer-
vescent explosion of feeling in which Maria and Oskar indulge:
'Da brach der Waldmeister wie ein Vulkan aus. Da kochte, ich
weiß nicht, wessen Volkes grünliche Wut' (p.223). Oskar
develops a 'third drumstick' and he asks himself the question:
'Hatte der Herr da unten seinen eigenen Kopf, eigenen Willen?'
(p.229).

In the post-war period reason is still vanquished by unreason
and this is made evident by the continued sexual dislocation of
Oskar and the characters who form his environment, and by the
recurrent imagery. By now it will be clear that one image is made
to link up with another, so much so that the one almost acts as
the substitute for the other, though obviously they are conditioned by the context in which they occur. Freudian simil-
arities emerge between tails, eels, fish, drumsticks, and even
patent-leather belts. The occurrence of one motif suggests all the

[14] David Roberts, 'Aspects of psychology and mythology in *Die Blechtrommel.
A study of the symbolic function of the "hero" Oskar*', in Manfred Jurgensen,
Grass: Kritik — Thesen — Analysen, (as in *12*), p.52.

occurrences of all the other motifs, as W.L. Sharfman[15] has indicated. A pattern of episodes also re-echoes throughout the novel. Once established in West Germany, for example, Oskar finds another cupboard and retreats into it, the cupboard in question belonging to Nurse Dorothea ('Im Kleiderschrank'). Oskar is reminded of the eels and the horse's head, and a patent-leather belt stimulates him into self-abuse (p.413). After the war Oskar makes a second visit to the fortifications on the Atlantic coast of France, and the title of the chapter itself ('Am Atlantik-wall oder es können die Bunker ihren Beton nicht loswerden') suggests that the attitudes and situations of the past are still to be encountered. Lankes, the former soldier who has now turned commercial artist, and Oskar 'celebrate' a meal of fish, whilst seated behind the bunker. Once again a sexual image, like that of the eels in 'Karfreitagskost', is employed. Inevitably Oskar is reminded of a previous meal which he and members of the circus company enjoyed shortly before the Allied invasion. The two companions, Oskar and Lankes, enter into a dispute about who should have the head or tail of the fish. The brutality in which Lankes indulged during the war has its counterpart in other acts of senseless cruelty which he now commits: he assaults his former lieutenant and rapes a nun. One comment which Oskar makes on the character and behaviour of Lankes is particularly revealing:

> Er kannte nur entweder oder, Kopf oder Schwanz, ertrunken oder gefallen. Mir nahm er die Zigaretten ab, den Oberleutnant warf er von der Düne, von meinem Fisch aß er, und einem Kind, das eigentlich dem Himmel geweiht war, zeigte er das Innere unseres Bunkers, malte, während sie noch in die offene See hinausschwamm, mit grobem, knolligem Fuß Bilder in die Luft... (p.458).

Lankes then goes on to make a profit out of his amorality by painting a series of pictures of nuns. Oskar condemns the actions of Lankes, though he shows a childish lack of

15 William L. Sharfman, 'The Organization of Experience in "The Tin Drum"', in *Minnesota Review*, Vol.6, 1966, pp.63-64.

differentiation by placing scrounging cigarettes and rape in the
same category of criminality. What appear initially to be
alternatives, emerge on closer analysis to be equally abhorrent
extremes. Through the mouth of Oskar, Grass condemns such
extremism and Lankes thereby joins the long line of characters
in Grass's works, whether this be Augst in *Aus dem Tagebuch
einer Schnecke* or the 'Endzielmänner' described in *Der Butt*
(p.44). Grass has referred to this kind of character in his essay
entitled significantly 'Begegnungen mit Kohlhaas' in his book
Der Bürger und seine Stimme. The sexual activities of Lankes
are reminiscent of the perverted personal relationships of the
various characters in the novel whether this be between Oskar
and Maria or Frau Greff or Schwester Dorothea, or between
Alexander Greff and his boyscouts or between Maria and
Matzerath. What applies to Jan Bronski and Agnes Matzerath is
also applicable to many of the characters in the novel:

> Die aßen alles selbst auf. Die hatten den großen Appetit,
> der nie aufhört, der sich selbst in den Schwanz beißt (p.80).

It is not coincidental that in the final chapters of the novel
Oskar finds a ring-finger, places it in a preserving jar and
proceeds to worship it, as though it were a holy shrine. Grass
makes plain the links between the various phallic symbols at a
previous stage in the novel, though he never supplies an
unambiguous interpretation of the imagery he employs:

> Gleichfalls versprachen mir die Zeichen auf Herberts
> Rücken zu jenem frühen Zeitpunkt schon den Ringfinger,
> und bevor mir Herberts Narben Versprechungen machten,
> waren es die Trommelstöcke, die mir vom dritten
> Geburtstag an die Narben, Fortpflanzungsorgane und
> endlich den Ringfinger versprachen. Doch muß ich noch
> weiter zurückgreifen: schon als Embryo, als Oskar noch
> gar nicht Oskar hieß, verhieß mir das Spiel mit meiner
> Nabelschnur nacheinander die Trommelstöcke, Herberts
> Narben, die gelegentlich aufbrechenden Krater jüngerer
> und älterer Frauen, schließlich den Ringfinger und immer

wieder, vom Gießkännchen des Jesusknaben an, mein
eigenes Geschlecht, das ich unentwegt, wie das launenhafte
Denkmal meiner Ohnmacht und begrenzten Möglichkeiten, bei mir trage (p.144).

Such images fulfil a prefigurative, configurative and
recapitulatory function within the novel and help to form a
thematic structure. They convey the subtlest of meaning, not
through explanatory discourses, but through association with
various episodes, interconnection, juxtaposition and
amplification. 'Kopf' and 'Schwanz' and the images which
cluster round them are examples of what Wellek and Warren
choose to call 'figuration', the 'oblique' discourse which
'partially compares worlds, precising its themes by giving them
translations into other idioms' (*26*, p.186). They give shape to
the amorality and immorality of the age through which Oskar
lives. The perverted sexuality is emblematic of the fractured
relationship between individuals, and suggests that unreason is
bring celebrated as the dominant force in the age through which
Oskar has been and is living. Oskar's fantasies are revelatory of
the unconscious mind of the narrator and the characters he
describes, as well as reflecting the collective unconscious of the
people to which he belongs. The imagery of head and tail
conjures up the idea that the values of Western civilisation and
those of Christianity have been corrupted and perverted: Goethe
has been undermined by Rasputin.

Another symbol which occurs in the novel is that of the unicorn, though it was constituted as a symbol long before Grass
chose to make use of it. Since the unicorn is a fabulous animal
with a horse's body and a single horn, the associations
connected with it also play a part in the network of correspondences surrounding the imagery of head and tail (it is a
horse's head which is eaten away by the eels, it must be
remembered). The *Duden-Lexikon* provides an intriguing
definition of the unicorn: 'Das Motiv der Einhornjagd (das
Einhorn ist nur zu fangen, wenn es in den Schoß einer Jungfrau
flüchtet) versinnbildlicht die Menschwerdung und jungfräuliche
Geburt Christi. Als Sinnbild der Keuschheit ist das Einhorn auch

Attribut für Maria.' As is evident from a close examination of the text, the women with whom Oskar comes into contact are all allusively linked with the Virgin Mary, either by direct reference or by their function in Oskar's life. They are all, according to Oskar, 'ladies on carpets who educate unicorns' (p.315). In perverted fashion, Oskar fulfils all the conditions demanded of a unicorn. He takes flight into the wombs of a succession of virgins and is trapped. Oskar embodies his needs in the image of woman. She flatters his irresponsibility and gratifies his desire for retreat, support and centre. She serves as a symbol of his evasion of responsibility and of his attempt to rid himself of feelings of guilt. In this sense Oskar may well be mirroring once again a basic attitude of his own time.

It is certainly true to say that Oskar turns to woman as a haven of refuge. He describes himself as wishing to escape from reality into a realm of prenatal purity and innocence. Born in the sign of Virgo he takes flight like the unicorn into the womb of a woman and is accordingly trapped. This is his experience with all the female characters in the novel. The grandmother first offers the tempting apple of escape and of cleanliness. Even Bronski flees from the harshness of reality in his liaison with Oskar's mother. Maria engulfs Oskar in the bourgeois world of National Socialism and in the arms of Lina Greff he is dragged down still further into the mire in an attempt to escape from Maria's influence. Roswitha Raguna offers her immortal body and the romantic sentimentality of the South as a possible escape route. The muse tempts Oskar with art as another variant on the theme of flight from reality. The nurse embodies for Oskar the mirage of purity. Oskar mirrors in his relations with women the tendency to indulge in emotional and by implication political escapism and in so doing to evade responsibility for one's own actions.

Another image which occurs in various forms throughout the novel is that of the roundabout. In a dream Oskar imagines himself seated as a child upon a roundabout which is kept in dizzy, perpetual motion by the figures of Goethe and Rasputin. Such a dream reveals the latent fears of Oskar, the narrator who highlights the intellectual and spiritual climate of his era. At the

same time we are made aware of the indulgent self-pity of
Oskar, who imagines the suffering of the children outweighs and
atones for the suffering of the Jews. Nevertheless, Goethe and
Rasputin conjure up the idea of a malevolent god who has made
possible the saturnalian inversion of all Christian principles. The
image of the roundabout gathers around it a complex of
associations by being linked nondiscursively with other images
and situations. Oskar is placed upon a revolving platform by the
Director of the Art Academy as the former tries to earn his living
as a model in the immediate post-war years, recalling the scene
when he was celebrated as a Messiah during the course of a black
mass, and emphasising that the roundabout of Goethe and
Rasputin has not stopped turning. The idea of circularity echoes
allusively in the course of Oskar's and Lankes's second visit to
the fortifications on the French coast. The imagery suggesting
circularity forms a mass of correspondences and insinuations,
which are rarely absent for long in the novel. The round shape of
the drum is, for example, frequently emphasised. The idea of
circularity and of futility is especially in evidence in the chapter
entitled 'Fortuna Nord' which describes Oskar's reversion to the
attitudes of the past in the altered circumstances of the present
and crystallises out in the image of 'Umbettung'. The ring-finger
also conjures up the idea of allegiance to the degenerate and
ossified values of the pre-1945 era. It suggests that the carnival
of the past still has an attractive appeal. One could also point to
the fact that the structure of the novel is circular: the novel starts
in a mental asylum and finishes in a mental asylum. As in the
historical sphere the eternal cycle of recurrence seems inevitable.
As we have mentioned in an earlier chapter, war sweeps across
Europe, and especially Danzig, with horrifying regularity,
necessitating in Oskar's native town a succession of 'Baumeister
und Abbruchunternehmer' (p.327). As Oskar observes in his
description of the Polish landscape, it seems created for the
activities of war:

> für die Schlacht, die schon dagewesen, die immer wieder
> kommt ... (p.21).

History presents itself, in Oskar's eyes, as an unbreakable chain of repetitiveness. This view of history underlies *Der Butt*, the novel which was published some eighteen years after *Die Blechtrommel*. Grass expresses the same idea, in the later novel, in terms of a fairy-tale, the pattern of which virtually determines the course of history: 'Die Märchen hören nur zeitweilig auf oder beginnen nach Schluß aufs Neue. Das ist die Wahrheit, jedesmal anders erzählt' (p.692). The fantasies of Oskar and the fairy-tales in *Der Butt* all have the quality of a nightmare, of a merry-go-round from which no escape seems possible: In reviewing the imagery of head and tail one is quickly aware of the fact that the imagery of circularity is one which gives shape to events on the personal plane as well as to events on the political plane. In fact the one may be regarded as an oblique reflection of the other. In this context one is reminded of Manfred Jurgensen's contention: 'Das Grass'sche Sprachbild ist eine Vergegenständlichung der historischen Erfahrung' (*11a*, p.18). Furthermore one is keenly aware of the fact that much of Grass's thinking is pictorial, that the image is the starting point for the novel — the sight of the boy playing the drum triggered off *Die Blechtrommel* — and that the imagery of the novel contributes to its coherence and forms a thematic framework. In this sense the imagery militates against and compensates for the ambiguity and ambivalence which are an inherent part of the narrative perspective.

6. The Chronological Framework

The other structure which holds the novel together is quite obviously the chronological framework. We have already noted the time-scale in accordance with which Oskar writes his autobiography. Sometimes reference to historical facts serves merely to fix events at a particular point in time: Oskar's grandfather, for example, meets his watery death:

> im Jahre dreizehn, also kurz bevor es losging (p.28);

and Mama and Matzerath get married:

> im Jahre dreiundzwanzig, da man für den Gegenwert einer Streichholzschachtel ein Schlafzimmer tapezieren, also mit Nullen mustern konnte... (p.33).

There is an offhand manner even about these two brief references to the historical background. Frequently historical or political details are introduced into the text in a deprecatory and ironical manner. For example, Jan Bronski is rejected for the army:

> was in jenen Zeiten, da man alles nur einigermaßen gerade Gewachsene nach Verdun schickte, um es auf Frankreichs Boden in die ewige Waagrechte zu bringen, allerlei über die Konstitution des Jan Bronski besagte (p.31).

Matzerath's acquisition of Party membership is couched in equally ironical terms:

> [Matzerath] trat im Jahre vierunddreißig, also verhältnismäßig früh die Kräfte der Ordnung erkennend, in die Partei ein und brachte es dennoch nur bis zum Zellenleiter (p.92).

The irony may be accompanied, as can be seen from these instances, by a satirical element. The black market in post-war Germany, which is the preparation for the economic miracle, is epitomised in the figure of Kurt Matzerath who shows great skill in exploiting a source of goods which are in short supply:

> Er hatte eine Quelle, verriet die Quelle aber nie, sagte jedoch immer wieder, selbst vorm Schlafengehen an Stelle eines Nachtgebetes: "Ich habe eine Quelle!" (p.360).

Here irony and satire are reinforced by a mildly fantastic element.

Political events are mentioned only cursorily and this applies to the examples we have quoted so far. Such a technique would seem to accord with the mode of presentation which Grass considers to be typical of Alfred Döblin: 'So setzt Döblin die Akzente: Sieg, Niederlage, Staatsaktionen, was immer sich datenfixiert als Dreißigjähriger Krieg niedergeschlagen hat, ist ihm einen Nebensatz, oft nur die bewußte Aussparung wert' (9, p.13). Thus we have the strange paradox that in *Die Blechtrommel* which Enzensberger categorises as 'a historical novel', political happenings are pushed to the periphery of the narrative. In this Grass follows the example of Döblin, his mentor, who regards history as an absurd process (9, p.8). The method Grass uses in *Die Blechtrommel* is the procedure which Döblin employs in *Wallenstein*: 'Die verstrickten Zeremonien listiger Vorbereitung in Wien, oder bei Hof des Maximilian von Bayern gesponnen, wälzen sich, verzerrt und wie vor Hohlspiegel gestellt, mystisch gesteigert über Seiten, während das Ergebnis höfischer Anstrengungen, sei es die Absetzung Wallensteins, sei es die Weigerung des sächsischen Kurfürsten, Gustav Adolf und sein Heer durch kursächsisches Land passieren zu lassen, lediglich mitgeteilt wird, betont achtlos, weil es nun mal dazu gehört; aber Geschichte, und das heißt die Vielzahl widersinniger und gleichzeitiger Abläufe, Geschichte, wie Döblin sie bloßstellen will, ist das nicht' (9, p.13). In *Die Blechtrommel* the defeat of the German armies in North Africa (p.261) or at Stalingrad (p.261) are treated in the same per-

functory fashion as the events of the Thirty Years' War in
Döblin's *Wallenstein*. The court intrigues and the armies' con-
fused search for winter quarters in Döblin's novel are replaced in
Grass's novel by the self-centred activities of the petit bourgeois.
Each separate sphere recaptures the atmosphere of history as a
confused mass of absurd and simultaneous trends. In *Die
Blechtrommel* the gulf between the grandiose political events
and the happenings being described is greater than in
Wallenstein, in that the social circles which Grass describes are
the at least ostensibly non-political sphere of the lower middle
class. Grass mentions the fact that in Grimmelshausen's
Simplicissimus Wallenstein does not appear; a similar situation
exists in *Die Blechtrommel*, for scant attention is paid, for
example, to Hitler in Grass's narrative: we are told that a picture
of Beethoven and one of Hitler hang on opposite walls of the
Matzerath sitting-room (see p.93 and p.149); and Hitler's entry
into Danzig (p.205) and his name (p.230) are mentioned in two
other contexts. As in Döblin's novel, the events in *Die
Blechtrommel* are presented in a distorted fashion as though
being viewed through a concave mirror. Grass reinforces his
analysis of Döblin's attitude to history by comparing Döblin's
with Schiller's presentation of the Thirty Years' War: 'Schiller
war bemüht, uns den Dreißigjährigen Krieg überschaubar
gegliedert darzustellen. Da ergibt sich eines aus dem anderen.
Seine ordnende Hand knüpft Bezüge, will Sinn geben. Das alles
zerschlägt Döblin mehrmals und bewußt zu Scherben, damit
Wirklichkeit entsteht' (9, p.14). The ordering hand which
imposes a pattern upon the current of political happenings is
absent in both Döblin's and Grass's novels, for both authors
regard history as an absurd process which does not serve any all-
embracing purpose. In *Die Blechtrommel* the events during the
Nazi regime and in the post-war era are not interconnected in
such a way that the reader is easily able to survey this period of
history as though from the historian's point of view. One event,
either in the political or in the personal sphere, does not proceed
from another. The thread of causality has been severed. Grass is
more concerned to capture the atmosphere of an era, and in
doing so he would claim that this is a realistic approach. Grass

proceeds in a manner which is similar to Grimmelshausen and Döblin: he leaves 'das große Schlachtgeschehen' aside, and chooses a viewpoint which is akin to 'die beschränkte Perspektive des tumben wie schlauen Überlebenden' (*9*, p.14).

The number of chapters in *Die Blechtrommel* which have as their content a major political event is very small: two in particular spring to mind, the *Kristallnacht* in which Jews were imprisoned or murdered and their businesses and synagogues set on fire; and the defence of the Polish Post Office. Only three other chapters could be represented as dealing primarily with political happenings — the Party rally as related in 'Die Tribüne', the experiences of the Jew in 'Desinfektionsmittel', and the expulsion of the Germans from Danzig in 'Wachstum im Güterwagen'. But in all these chapters the perspective is that of the ingenuous child who can see only what affects him directly. Furthermore, satirical and fantastic elements rule out the possibility of a factual account or of demonstrating causal relationships. The chapter entitled 'Glaube Hoffnung Liebe', for example, takes the form of a nightmarish fairy-tale which reaches its climax in the sentences:

Ein ganzes leichtgläubiges Volk glaubte an den Weihnachtsmann. Aber der Weihnachtsmann war in Wirklichkeit der Gasmann (p.164).

The defence of the Polish Post Office culminates in Jan Bronski building a delicately balanced house of cards, an image which suggests that Jan is totally divorced from reality, scarcely able to comprehend what is going on around him. The other fact that would seem to militate against the claim that *Die Blechtrommel* is a 'historical novel' is, of course, the fact that Grass does not deal with those circles in which political decisions are made, but situates his action exclusively in the social environment of the lower middle class. Geno Hartlaub[16] quotes Grass as saying that in *Die Blechtrommel* he has tried to show ' "wie latent politisch die unpolitischen kleinbürgerlichen Schichten als Träger einer

[16] Geno Hartlaub, 'Wir, die wir übriggeblieben sind...', in Gert Loschütz (ed.), *Von Buch zu Buch — Günter Grass in der Kritik*, as in *3*, p.212.

Weltanschauung wie die des NS-Regimes gewesen sind''.
Besonders in Deutschland haben die Arbeiter den Hang zum
Kleinbürgertum mit seinen Verwaschenheiten, seiner Hybris und
seinen allgemein bekannten Eigenschaften, die im privaten
Bereich liebenswert sein können, aber gefährlich oder grotesk
werden, wenn dies Kleinbürgertum die politische Führung
ergreift'. Günter Grass has thus made it clear that he consciously
restricted the choice of his material to the world of the petit
bourgeoisie and that this personal sphere is intended to reflect
the national sphere; though it would be wrong, I think, to equate
the personal directly with the national sphere. The eccentric
narrative perspective makes such a direct equation difficult and
leads to an artificial interpretation. The result is that the reader
forces the novel into an allegorical strait-jacket, although Grass
has denied that his novel can be understood in terms of an
allegory. As in the case of Döblin, events are reflected in
distorted fashion, as though 'through a concave mirror'.

Nevertheless events on the personal plane are linked with
events on the political or military plane, and the activities in the
sphere of politics or war are thereby belittled and made to look
ridiculous. An obvious example can be found in Oskar's affair
with Lina Greff:

> Vjazma und Brjansk; dann setzte die Schlammperiode ein.
> Auch Oskar begann, Mitte Oktober einundvierzig kräftig
> im Schlamm zu wühlen. Man mag mir nachsehen, daß ich
> den Schlammerfolgen der Heeresgruppe Mitte meine
> Erfolge im unwegsamen und gleichfalls recht schlammigen
> Gelände der Frau Lina Greff gegenüberstelle. Ähnlich wie
> sich dort, kurz vor Moskau, Panzer und LKW's fest-
> fuhren, fuhr ich mich fest (p.250).

Maria's and Oskar's liaison unfolds, whilst Fritz Truczinski
makes a tour of the Western capitals in 1940 (p.221). Sherbet
becomes the 'objective correlative' for the explosion of feeling
which on the national level was a characteristic feature of
German political irrationality during the Nazi period (see also
p.61 of Chapter 5): Maria and Oskar delight in the effervescence

of sherbet in Maria's cupped hand. In this context the word 'Volk', which for the Nazis had such an evocative appeal, is introduced nonchalantly into the narrative, as though it had scarcely any contribution to make to the general meaning of the passage, and Oskar even includes a negative to accentuate the offhand manner:

> Da kochte, ich weiß nicht, wessen Volkes grünliche Wut (p.223).

Their amorous experiments enter a second phase, in which Oskar pours the sherbet into Maria's navel and adds his saliva so that an eruption of volcanic proportions can take place:

> und als es in dem Krater zu kochen anfing, verlor Maria alle für einen Protest nötigen Argumente: denn der kochend brausende Bauchnabel hatte der hohlen Hand viel voraus (p.228).

Here, as in other parts of the novel, the grotesque relationships between man and woman are sometimes used to emphasise the extent to which real love is absent from their lives — Maria's and Matzerath's love-making would be an example of this — but they are also employed as a means of reducing political and military affairs to the level of the ridiculous.

The theme of explosiveness seems in the third book of the novel to satirise the German economic miracle. The passionate feeling which characterises Oskar's and Maria's amorous adventures during the war has its counterpart in the post-war period in the insistent demand for happiness. Oskar describes his overpowering desire for happiness as he sits eating his breakfast:

> und verspürte, auf etwas Knorpel im Speck beißend, jäh und bis in die Ohrenränder ein Bedürfnis nach Glück, gegen alles bessere Wissen wollte ich Glück, alle Skepsis wog nicht das Verlangen nach Glück auf, hemmungslos glücklich wollte ich werden... (p.366),

and later:

> Wie ein Vulkan brach das Glück aus... (p.368).

Accordingly Oskar sets out to find happiness. He is employed as a stonemason who inscribes tombstones. In this capacity he makes a living out of death. The personal quest for happiness finds its image on the economic and national plane in the power-station which is incessantly engaged in explosive activity:

> Das neue, zischende, immer explodieren wollende Kraftwerk Fortuna Nord (p.378).

The power-station erupts with the same venomous force ('Kraft') as do Korneff's boils, those 'Verhärtungen' (see p.371) which eject their poison at periodic intervals, in this instance against the background of snippets from the Lord's Prayer. The power-station rises up into the air like a phallus and thus one is reminded of the other phallic emblems to which Oskar draws our attention, for example, the ring-finger which he discovers whilst transferring a corpse from one graveyard to another. The nationalism of the pre-1945 period has been succeeded by the materialism of the post-war era. The parallelism between personal and national events, the imagery and the associations which are both backward and forward looking, obscenity and to a lesser extent blasphemy, all combine to serve the purpose of satirical reduction.

Many of the happenings on the personal level can be related to the historical and political framework. The way Matzerath meets his death, for example, comes to symbolise the collapse of Nazi Germany: the shopkeeper and cook from the lower middle class, whose attitudes assisted Hitler to power, chokes in an attempt to swallow his Nazi Party badge and is riddled through with bullets from a Russian machine-gun. Agnes Matzerath's death takes place against the deteriorating relations between Germany and Poland, and signifies more importantly, as we have suggested already, the triumph of unreason over reason. Greff's suicide on the gigantic, elaborately constructed drumming machine occurs in October 1942, shortly after the German occupation of Stalingrad (see p.254). The nihilistic activities of the dusters ('Die Stäuber') are being undertaken whilst Paris is being evacuated and when the Germans have retreated to the Vistula (Oskar expresses the historical fact in a more ironical form: 'Nach langem Lauf kam die Heeresgruppe Mitte an der Weichsel zum Stehen' (pp.304-05)). They indulge in destructiveness for its own sake, are referred to as 'Halb-wüchsige' and swear allegiance on the drum to a saviour who possesses a miraculous weapon, a glass-cutting voice, in the same way that at that time Hitler was launching his miraculous weapons, his V1s and V2s, against Britain. They seem to epitomise the total breakdown of all civilised values and they can in any case be related to the gangs of youths such as the 'Edelweißpiraten' who did in fact exist at that time. Given these facts, it seems doubtful whether they should be compared with the members of the July conspiracy against Hitler, as is suggested by Georg Just.[17] In all such instances the events of the time are deprived of their grandeur, trivialised and made to look sordid. Oskar himself is not a satirist: Grass employs him as the ironic or satiric device for exposing events and attitudes to ridicule, the principal method being that of interconnecting elements which are incongruous, thus producing a comic combined with an alienating effect. Even in the episode entitled 'Die Tribüne' Oskar does not emerge as a satirist, he is not presented as an opponent of National Socialism. He is largely indifferent to any form of political belief. Nevertheless he breaks up the Party rally, wittingly or unwittingly, and is the medium through which this political gathering is made to look ludicrous, in that the participants all finish up by dancing the Charleston and disappearing, suitably paired, into the nearby woodland. However, there is one occasion when Oskar does set himself up as a satirist in his own right and that is in the chapter entitled 'Glaube Hoffnung Liebe'.

The more usual situation is that Grass, the satirist, dons the mask of Oskar, the narrator, in order to unmask others. One has

[17] Georg Just, *Darstellung und Appell in der Blechtrommel von Günter Grass*, (Frankfurt/M, Athenäum Verlag, 1972), p.180.

to bear in mind that the dividing line between irony and satire is fluid and that, as Northrop Frye has said, satire is militant irony. The cyclic view of history, which is apparent in the novel, diminishes the satiric impact as does the ambiguity inherent in the narrative perspective. There is also some truth in Enzensberger's observation (see *6*) — at least in respect of this novel — that Grass lacks the moral instinct of the true satirist as well as the absurd hope that the state of the world can be changed. Nevertheless there are satirical elements in *Die Blechtrommel* and more especially in the third book of the novel. There the satiric thrust is directed at the continuity of the German development, at those modes of thinking and feeling which constituted the solid substratum for the Nazi ideology and which still exist today, though possibly in a modified, but not necessarily fundamentally altered, form. We have already noted that the fervour with which nationalistic ideals were pursued during the Nazi period is the fervour which gave rise to the German economic miracle: one miracle has been replaced by another. Through the medium of Oskar, Grass denounces the inability of German society to come to terms with the past. Such lack of orientation can be seen expressed in a number of ways. The art students, for example, revel in accusation of such a generalised nature that they overlook the details of history. Their teacher, Professor Kuchen, a kind of artistic Rasputin, whose only colour seems to be black, claims that expression is all and maintains that Oskar

> drücke das zerstörte Bild des Menschen anklagend, herausfordernd, zeitlos und dennoch den Wahnsinn unseres Jahrhunderts ausdrückend aus,

Then he proceeds to issue the instruction:

> "Zeichnet ihn nicht, den Krüppel, schlachtet ihn, kreuzigt ihn, nagelt ihn mit Kohle aufs Papier!" (p.383).

The art students recognise Oskar's deformity, the malformation which took place when, at the end of the war, he attempted to renounce his drum, and yet they encourage him in his immaturity. They delight in despair and pessimism, and in this sense are as divorced from reality as those who suppress all knowledge of the past. They force him once again into the role of Christ, or Antichrist, which he may or may not wish to adopt. One of the art students, Raskolnikoff, who, as one might expect, is somewhat obsessed by guilt and atonement, forces the drum upon Oskar and thus resurrects once more the barrier between Oskar and reality (p.392). A short time later Oskar celebrates the resurrection of his drum, and he and Klepp found a jazz band.

Oskar's attitude to art, which is his name for beating a drum, is just as suspect as that of the art students and art professor or that of Lankes. As we have noted, Lankes converts his own inhumanity into art. Oskar claims in the same context that 'his art also cries out for bread':

> es galt, die Erfahrungen des dreijährigen Blechtrommlers Oskar während der Vorkriegs- und Kriegszeit mittels der Blechtrommel in das pure, klingende Gold der Nachkriegs-zeit zu verwandeln (p.459).

Oskar intends to cling to the childish viewpoint and this is to be the source of inspiration for his art. In keeping with his creed, he reduces the customers in Schmuh's Onion Cellar to the level of children: he suffers the little children to come unto him. He has them behave like children:

> Alte Wege trommelte ich hin und zurück, machte die Welt aus dem Blickwinkel der Dreijährigen deutlich, nahm die zur wahren Orgie unfähige Nachkriegsgesellschaft zuerst an die Leine, was heißen soll, ich führte sie in den Posadowskiweg, in Tante Kauers Kindergarten, hatte sie schon soweit, daß sie die Unterkiefer hängenließen, sich bei den Händchen nahmen, die Fußspitzen einwärts schoben, mich, ihren Rattenfänger erwarteten (p.444).

In this chapter, 'Im Zwiebelkeller', post-war German society is

shown to be characterised by immaturity and by 'the inability to
mourn', to use the title of Mitscherlich's book. Oskar allows
himself to be employed by a concert agency which is organised
by Meister Bebra. He sets out on tours of West Germany and
entertains large audiences with solo performances on his drum.
The publicity campaign builds him up as a magician, a faith-
healer (a word which was used originally in conjunction with
Rasputin) and as a Messiah. Once again Oskar enters into the
role of the Messiah, suggesting that he is reverting to the habits
of the pre-1945 period. The audiences react in the manner of
three-year-olds when Oskar relates episodes from the life of the
miraculous Rasputin on his drum (p.463). The merry-go-round
set in motion by Goethe and Rasputin keeps on turning;
circularity still holds sway. Infantilism is still presented as the
disease of German society and as a sign that the members of the
Federal Republic are inclined to suppress the uncomfortable
facts connected with National Socialism. In the light of Oskar's
activity as a drummer in post-war Germany it is easy to
understand Hanspeter Brode's assessment of *Die Blechtrommel*
as a protest against the widespread tendency to suppress the Nazi
period (5, p.92).

Grass also attacks the continuity of German political thinking
in the chapter entitled 'Die letzte Straßenbahn oder Anbetung
eines Weckglases'. Oskar describes how two men have arrested
Viktor Weluhn, who was involved in the defence of the Polish
Post Office but managed to escape, and how they try to shoot
him in accordance with an order of execution issued in 1939.
Only the fantastic intervention of Oskar saves 'poor Victor'
from death and perhaps introduces a mildly optimistic note in
the course of this condemnation of the German attitude towards
Poland. This is obviously not the first time in the book that
Grass attacks the German treatment of Poland. On one
occasion, for example, Oskar makes an ironic comment on the
Great Powers' tendency to divide up Poland (p.328). The
massive military onslaught on the Polish Post Office contains an
implied criticism of the German behaviour to Poland. Hanspeter
Brode has drawn attention to a statement which Grass has made
about Poland and in which he explains 'daß mich die deutsche,

an Polen begangene Schuld bei meiner Arbeit als Schriftsteller
entscheidend bestimmt hat' (5, p.99).

7. *The Theme of Guilt*

In an interview with Heinz Ludwig Arnold, Günter Grass has stated the four main points of comparison between the three works which comprise the Danzig Trilogy. The first similarity which he singles out is the theme of guilt: 'Alle drei Ich-Erzähler in allen drei Büchern schreiben aus Schuld heraus: aus verdrängter Schuld, aus ironisierter Schuld, im Fall Matern aus pathetischem Schuldverlangen, einem Schuldbedürfnis — das ist das erste Gemeinsame' (*1*, pp.10-11). Elsewhere Grass speaks of Oskar's 'fingierte Schuld' and 'seine wirklichen Verschuldungen'.

It is not difficult to locate Oskar's simulated guilt. The narrator, an inveterate impostor, claims on one occasion to have murdered his mother and his uncle. He starts off his confession by producing the preposterous claim that his drum committed the murders, and then replaces this pretence by an ostensibly more honest, but in reality just as fantastic a statement:

> ... meine Trommel, nein, ich selbst, der Trommler Oskar, brachte zuerst meine arme Mama, dann den Jan Bronski, meinen Onkel und Vater ins Grab (p.201).

Oskar even makes this pair of murders into a list by adding the names of Roswitha Raguna and Matzerath. He produces this confession in the presence of Meister Bebra who has set himself up as his judge and who, according to Oskar, plays his role excellently (p.461). Oskar presumably does not want to spoil this fine piece of theatre and plays his part equally well, for he confesses all.

The theme of guilt once again figures largely in the final chapter of the novel. However, Oskar's feelings of guilt do not relate to a specific aspect of reality. On the one hand Oskar admits that he is pretending to be afraid — he speaks of 'das mühsame Aufrechterhalten der Furcht' (p.486) — and on the other hand his behaviour is that of a child — he is afraid of a kind of bogeyman, the so-called 'Schwarze Köchin' — and in addition the children's game in which this witch occurs involves a child being singled out, even though the child concerned, as A. Leslie Willson[18] points out, is 'superficially innocent while paradoxically revealed in a state of terrible guilt'. Oskar, the confidence trickster, is bound to conceal the nature of his guilt. As is the case in assessing any ironical statement, it is up to the reader to assess where the truth lies. The situation in *Hundejahre* is much less ambivalent, in that it is quite clear that Matern is trying to disguise the fact that he assaulted his Jewish friend: he cannot accept the reality of his own past. In *Katz und Maus* it could also be maintained that the narrator has no adequate understanding of what National Socialism entailed. Both suffer from a kind of moral blindness, a huge incapacity to recall any embarrassing or uncomfortable facts from their own past or from the past of the nation to which they belong. Few verifiable facts are known about the character of Oskar. Only one thing stands out as absolutely incontestable: he retreats behind the mask of a child at the age of three and persists in this attitude even when he has reached the age of thirty, when one might expect the adult outlook to predominate. It is significant that in his game with Meister Bebra Oskar purchases the forgiveness of his father-confessor by signing a document. According to the contract he is obliged to undertake a series of concerts which will consist of solo performances on his drum. He explains the arrangements in the following terms:

> Manch einer mag nun glauben, daß jener Vertrag in doppelter Ausfertigung, den ich zweimal unterschrieb, meine Seele erkaufte oder Oskar zu schrecklichen Missetaten verpflichtete. Nichts davon! Als ich mit Hilfe des Dr. Dösch im Vorzimmer den Vertrag studierte, verstand ich schnell und mühelos, daß Oskars Aufgabe darin bestand, alleine mit seiner Blechtrommel vor dem

[18] A. Leslie Willson, 'The Grotesque Everyman in Günter Grass's "Die Blechtrommel"', in *Monatshefte*, Vol.LVIII, No.2, 1966, p.132.

Publikum aufzutreten, daß ich so trommeln mußte, wie ich
es als Dreijähriger getan hatte und später noch einmal in
Schmuhs Zwiebelkeller. Die Konzertagentur verpflichtete
sich, meine Tourneen vorzubereiten, erst einmal auf die
Werbetrommel zu schlagen, bevor "Oskar der Trommler"
mit seinem Blech auftrat (p.462).

The signing of the document marks the dividing line between the
world of fantasy, i.e. the game of make-believe in which Bebra
as father-confessor and judge and Oskar as penitent sinner
indulge, and the world of reality. Whether the contract can
legitimately be compared with a pact with the devil — and Oskar
carefully denies that this is so — is debatable; the agreement the
two of them draw up, however, is something quite specific. We
know that Oskar can carry out the contract, that is, he can beat
his drum as a three-year-old, and we also know that the effect is
that he reduces nominal adults to the level of children, and we
shall also find out shortly that he does abide by the agreement.
By referring to the surrender of his soul and the terrible
misdeeds, Oskar tries to belittle what he does achieve and divert
attention from it. The contract accurately describes Oskar's
situation: he is to encourage members of the public to remain
infantile in their emotional reactions and in their behaviour, the
agency having prepared the audiences for his appearances.
Publicity would have him regarded as a magician and Messiah,
and thus an image is imposed upon him. Oskar moulds society
and society moulds him. He encourages the public in its
immaturity and its escapism. As in the pre-1945 period Oskar
places the drum between himself and reality. In the same way the
drum becomes a barrier between individuals and historical
reality, whether this be of the present or of the past. Oskar
effectively prevents society from understanding its past and
coming to terms with it. He enjoys being mindless, is encouraged
to be so and infects society with the same degree of
irresponsibility. This is his guilt: he flees from reality and
persuades others to follow his example. They persist in the

Unwissenheit ..., die damals in Mode kam und noch heute
manchem als flottes Hütchen zu Gesicht steht (p.202).

Conclusion

In *Die Blechtrommel* Grass establishes Oskar as the ingenuous narrator and then withdraws completely, ostensibly leaving the narrator in sole charge. The latter tells his story from an assumed, an ironical point of view, pretending to be either a child or a madman or both simultaneously. Our author never interferes directly in the story-telling, but he does allow Oskar to unmask himself. Sometimes the imagery serves to break through the narrator's barrier of pretence and deceit. Of course, there are occasions when the reader is not sure whether Grass himself might not be undermining his narrator by allowing discrepancies to appear of which his narrator is unaware. In other words, the reader is frequently unsure whether an utterance or a word is intentionally or unconsciously ironical. Sometimes Oskar takes the reader into his confidence and openly states that he is lying or exaggerating. On other occasions Oskar's statements are contradictory: there is a discrepancy between appearance and reality. Frequently, however, the narrator playfully ironises himself or is ironised by some form of exaggeration, a flight of fancy, an innuendo, ambiguity or other stylistic warning signal. Hence doubt is systematically cultivated in the mind of the reader to the point where he is more or less unable to take any of Oskar's statements at their face value, even where stylistic warning signals seem to be absent. However, even though the reader has no sure grip on empirical reality, at least two elements constitute stabilising factors within the novel: the imagery and the chronological framework of political events.

Wayne C. Booth (see *2*) draws attention to the fact that generations of readers have found themselves wondering whether Joyce was ironising the hero in *The Portrait of the Artist as a Young Man*. There is a similar element of uncertainty in *Die Blechtrommel*. Oskar hides behind his mask, refusing to allow any real insight into his character, and preferring concealment and dissembling to the adult obligation for accepting moral and political responsibility. One asks oneself whether it is the author's intention to expose to ridicule Oskar's flight from reality, believing that this has a generalised application to twentieth-century Germany, or whether Oskar's escapism is a necessary but incidental factor in the kind of narrative perspective which Grass has chosen to employ. It would appear, however, that Oskar's pose is motivated by his desire for psychological facelessness and moral and political irresponsibility. He wishes in effect to cover up his own sense of guilt by refusing to reveal his own character and by blaming individuals and circumstances for his own shortcomings. In this sense one could legitimately claim that Oskar has a representative function to fulfil, even though he is an oblique and ironic expression of the trends of his time.

Oskar undermines truth and thus creates an atmosphere of doubt and ambivalence. His plunge into the 'darkest abyss of romance' is paralleled by the destruction of reason, which reaches its culmination in National Socialist Germany, as described in *Die Blechtrommel*. All characters pay homage to the cult of unreason which is suggested by the associations connected with Rasputin and by the imagery of head and tail. The imagery serves to throw into relief the corruption of truth, morality and Christianity which is the decisive characteristic of the society to which Oskar belongs. There are no positive values within the novel and accordingly the characters are not motivated by ethical considerations. The relationships between men and women in the novel are sordid: the love-play of all the characters is ludicrous and grotesque. The characters' irrational behaviour, their allegiance to unbridled emotion, finds its counterpart in an amorality of situation, and also in the circularity of the plot. In the world that Oskar describes, decisions are no longer determined by moral considerations. He depicts a world in which choice is no longer meaningful, in which alternatives are equally abhorrent, equally amoral, equally inhuman in their effects. This fact is reflected in the basic absurdity and abnormality of the human situations which are depicted in the novel. The complete lack of moral, religious or philosophical principles within the novel, and the absence of truth as an ideal to which men aspire, are conditioned to a large extent by the narrative perspective. Oskar, the narrator, views, or pretends to view, Nazism and the post-war period through the eyes of a child, in other words, he sees an immoral age through amoral eyes. In this process all values are fantastically inverted. Oskar indulges in a carnival of amorality and infantilism which is paralleled by the grim saturnalian eruption of National Socialism and in the hedonism of the post-war economic miracle. The narrator describes what Grass[19] has elsewhere chosen to call 'die blinde amoralische Realität mit ihren elementaren Interessen'. He mirrors the psychological, moral and political atmosphere of his time in grotesque and distorted fashion. Kurt Lothar Tank maintains in his book 'daß in ... Oskar der Geist und Ungeist einer Epoche beschworen ist' (*23*, p.8). Oskar gives shape to the amorality of the age through which he lives. He reflects in fractured manner the extent to which truth, morality and religion have been eroded under the impact of bourgeois attitudes and politics.

The introduction of the egocentric, amoral and highly imaginative narrator allows that degree of alienation and detachment which is the basic precondition for Grass's ironical, and sometimes satirical, survey of the German development. Oskar, the flawed reflector of reality, permits the reader to view the world from an unusual angle and hence sharpens his perception of the real world, as he, the reader, understands it from his own experience or from his own reading of outside sources. The ironist, using Oskar as his narrator, does not describe the realities of the world in objective terms but produces what is often a grotesque travesty of the situation. The ironic viewpoint and the world of fantasy which Oskar describes direct our attention to actuality and prompt us to decode the irony and the grotesque, and to draw comparisons between the fantastic and the real world. There is constant interplay between these two worlds in the mind of the reader, and from this interaction the critical attitude is fostered. The fantasy and the naive attitude of

[19] Günter Grass, *Über das Selbstverständliche* (Neuwied, Luchterhand, 1968), p.175.

the childish narrator serve as a means of abstracting the characters from their usual setting and thus exposing them to our critical gaze. The irony, the satire and the grotesque sharpen our critical awareness.

In ambivalent manner Oskar epitomises the German outlook, whilst Danzig is the microcosm of Germany. In this sense then *Die Blechtrommel* is a historical novel, yet one in which political events are mentioned in a casual, take-it-or-leave-it manner. As in the case of the film the novel emerges as a grotesque lament for the grievous wrongs perpetrated against the Poles and the Jews and an expression of the sense of deprivation which proceeds from the expulsion of the Germans from Danzig. At the same time *Die Blechtrommel* constitutes an oblique criticism of the German development, on occasions a bitter satirical attack on the continuity of German political attitudes and actions.

The combination of laughter and tears, which in varying degrees is the common feature of irony, satire and the grotesque, allow the reader to see a period of time in perspective. Thus the author avoids the serious, realistic portrayal of this epoch which the reader would find overwhelmingly oppressive. The grotesque in particular has both a liberating effect as well as causing anxiety. This tight-rope walk which involves both the release and the creation of tension might well be one of the few ways of coming to terms with the past. In this way Günter Grass finds with *Die Blechtrommel* an effective and meaningful vehicle for 'Vergangenheitsbewältigung', whilst at the same time producing a novel which because of the open-ended nature of irony is extremely stimulating and calls upon the reader's independent and active involvement.

Finally, a brief comparison between Thomas Mann's *Doktor Faustus* and *Die Blechtrommel* may serve to highlight the salient features of Grass's novel. Henry Hatfield has pointed to the appropriateness and the hazardous nature of such an under-taking: 'Perhaps some day some bold fellow will note an analogy between *Die Blechtrommel* and *Doktor Faustus*, though this would probably annoy both Herr Grass and the revered shade of Thomas Mann' (*10*, p.125). However, it must be stated that Grass himself has never drawn a comparison between his first novel and *Doktor Faustus*, though he has acknowledged his indebtedness to *Moby Dick*, *Simplicissimus*, *Wilhelm Meister* and *Der grüne Heinrich* (see 7). Furthermore Grass has stoutly denied that his novel is allegorical, whilst Mann and his interpreters have never ceased making such claims for *Doktor Faustus*. The latter, so T.J. Reed claims, 'attempts the impossible: to encompass and explain the German catastrophe' (see *20*, p.360). He ventures to embark, as Freud might have said, upon the pathology of a cultural community. Grass, it could be maintained, sets himself a similarly impossible task, particularly if one recalls Kurt Lothar Tank's statement that Grass conjures up the 'spirit of an epoch' in *Die Blechtrommel* (*23*, p.8). There is a difference in time-span: *Doktor Faustus* conjures up the period of Luther, though concentrating on the years of Leverkühn's life from 1885 to 1945, whilst *Die Blechtrommel* covers the time from 1899 to 1954. Both focus upon National Socialism and its origins, though Grass does establish an element of continuity beyond the great divide of 1945. In their different ways Mann and Grass build into their novels 'das ungebrochene Weiterleben des Alten im Neuen'.[20] Continuity is an inescapable factor in German history for both of them. Mann started his literary career by describing in *Buddenbrooks* the 'Verfall einer Familie', whilst his final major work was to adumbrate the decline of a community. Grass in his first novel places the decline of a family side by side with the disintegration of a national community.

Mann and Grass share a traditional feature of the German novel: the fact that art and artist have frequently been a focal point around which the novel has been constructed. Earlier works of Thomas Mann concentrate upon the relationship between art, the artist and the bourgeois, as in *Tonio Kröger* and *Der Tod in Venedig*. In *Doktor Faustus* the artist becomes the seismograph of society: the elements in the cultural and political decline of his national community are traced through the

---

[20] Karlheinz Hasselbach, *Thomas Mann: Doktor Faustus* (Munich, R. Oldenbourg Verlag, 1977), p.31.

medium of his life and his work. However, Mann does not
consider the man of letters, but rather the musician, to be the
typical representative of German art and indeed of Germany,
and makes the following claims about music in a speech entitled
'Deutschland und die Deutschen':

> Die Musik ist dämonisches Gebiet ... berechnetste
> Ordnung und chaosträchtige Wider-Vernunft zugleich ...
> die der Wirklichkeit fernste und zugleich die
> passionierteste der Künste, abstrakt und mystisch. Soll
> Faust der Repräsentant der deutschen Seele sein, so müßte
> er musikalisch sein; denn abstrakt und mystisch, das heißt
> musikalisch, ist das Verhältnis des Deutschen zur Welt, —
> das Verhältnis eines dämonisch angehauchten Professors,
> ungeschickt und dabei von dem hochmütigen Bewußtsein
> bestimmt, der Welt an "Tiefe" überlegen zu sein.[21]

Whether such a statement is factually correct, is obviously
debatable and virtually irrelevant, for Mann employs music as a
means of expressing the situation of art, culture and man in
general. In *Die Blechtrommel* we are also confronted with the
life of a musician, Oskar the drummer, grotesque and much
reduced in physical and cultural stature. The drum is the
amusing and parodistic device for symbolising Oskar's
relationship to the world. The drum is not only indicative of his
lack of emotional maturity but also conditions the reaction of
the adult world to the drummer himself.

Adrian Leverkühn is intended to represent the German soul
and Germany itself. Yet in no way is he implicated in the
political developments of his time. There are no causal
relationships between his life and the political life of Germany.
Mann works, not with direct connections, but with parallels. As
T.J. Reed states, 'the temptations an artist was exposed to by his
times were identical at their source with those which endangered
political society' (*20*, p.364). Oskar stands in the same relationship to the events of his time as does Adrian Leverkühn —

[21] Thomas Mann, *Deutschland und die Deutschen* (Stockholm, Bermann-
Fischer Verlag, 1947), p.15.

neither of them is a politician. Yet they both encapsulate the spirit of an age. Thomas Mann bases his analysis of the German catastrophe on the principle that social trends and political happenings have their roots in the psychology of individuals, in the collective consciousness of a people. Serenus Zeitblom, the narrator in *Doktor Faustus*, provides the reader with the appropriate theoretical orientation:

> Bei einem Volk von der Art des unsrigen... ist das Seelische immer das Primäre und eigentlich Motivierende; die politische Aktion ist zweiter Ordnung, Reflex, Ausdruck, Instrument (*14*, p.472).

In *Doktor Faustus* the narrator (Serenus Zeitblom) and the Faustian musician (Adrian Leverkühn) have separate identities, though they do come close to being a Doctor Jekyll and Mr Hyde combination. These two characters are accompanied in the novel by a collection of individuals who likewise recreate the temper of their age. In this sense they are not individuals at all but perform rather a symbolic function. Mann refers to one particular group of people, the so-called Munich Circle, as 'ein wunderliches Aquarium von Geschöpfen der Endzeit'.[22] Such a description could be applied with not too much difficulty to the collection of characters — or caricatures — who parade before us in *Die Blechtrommel*. Reservations would merely attach themselves to the word 'Endzeit', since Grass's novel goes beyond the year zero. Personal tragedy in *Doktor Faustus* prefigures or configures national tragedy. The breakdown of Clarissa Rodde's relationship with her French fiancé, for example, anticipates the severing of Franco-German relations. Yet Mann locates his characters in the upper-middle-class intellectual circles of Germany, whilst Grass situates his characters firmly in the petit-bourgeois environment, the typical inhabitant of which is the shopkeeper. Mann focuses his attention upon the climate of the epoch by describing intellectual discussions and by analysing the musical works of Adrian

---

[22] Thomas Mann, *Die Entstehung des Doktor Faustus* (Amsterdam, Bermann-Fischer/Querido-Verlag, 1949), p.178.

Leverkühn. In keeping with his thoroughly Germanic understanding of the novel, Thomas Mann 'transforms outward into
inward events' (*18*, p.258). Günter Grass on the other hand
reverses this process, dispenses with abstract argumentations
and moves fairly and squarely into the realm of the anecdotal.
He deals not with monumental 'Geschichte', but with personal
'Geschichten', though the latter illuminate indirectly the former.

Both novels are united by yet another feature in that they both
treat the theme of irrationalism as being central to the understanding of the German dilemma, a theme which according to
Roy Pascal gives special shape to the German novel (see *18*,
p.297). In *Doktor Faustus* the musical hero who treads with
equal fervour in the footsteps of Faust and Nietzsche seeks to
break away from self-doubt and sterility by a pact with the
Devil, the spirit not of scepticism and self-questioning, but the
source of enthusiasm and passionate involvement. He allies
himself with unreason, with the 'Wider-Vernunft' of a previous
quotation, though Adrian's act of syphilitic self-infection
antedates his interview with the Devil. Oskar and the characters
in *Die Blechtrommel* allow moderation to be swept aside by
passion: theirs is a headless and unreasoned plunge into
mindlessness. The image of the head being eaten away by eels is
an entirely appropriate expression of this process. The
counterpart in *Doktor Faustus* is the sexual disease which
deprives its victim of his powers of thinking and results in
madness and ultimately death. Oskar's abandonment to
Rasputin and Adrian's to Dionysos are paralleled by their
country's surrender to irrationalism and inhumanity. Morality
has been defeated in its battle with aesthetics. It is interesting,
though possibly purely coincidental, that in both novels the
word 'Falter' has a role to play: in *Doktor Faustus* 'Falter' is
linked by association with the prostitute who predisposes Adrian
Leverkühn to the demonic realm of music, whereas in *Die
Blechtrommel* a moth inclines Oskar to music.

The two books differ in their attitude to the demonic. In
Doktor Faustus the course of German history is invested with
the seductive appeal of the grandiose and the metaphysical. The
fascination of the Faust myth is unabated. Even if one allows for

the tongue in the cheek — and that presupposes that one knows the extent of the allowance — the concluding paragraph of *Doktor Faustus* does envisage evil on the grand Wagnerian scale:

> Deutschland, die Wangen hektisch gerötet, taumelte dazumal auf der Höhe wüster Triumphe, im Begriffe, die Welt zu gewinnen kraft des einen Vertrages, den es zu halten gesonnen war, und den es mit seinem Blute gezeichnet hatte....

The ghosts of Faust and Wagner have not been laid to rest. In *Die Blechtrommel* Grass leaves much less room for historical uncertainty. The devil, metaphorically speaking (for he is scarcely allowed to appear in person), is unceremoniously knocked off his pedestal. National Socialism is deprived of its aura of grandeur. Grass goes in for sordid, squalid reality. The demise of Nazism is visualised in terms of a shopkeeper choking on his own Party badge. The demon of German history is exorcised.

Nevertheless *Doktor Faustus* emerges in the last resort as a lament, in the same way that Leverkühn's final musical composition, 'D. Fausti Weheklag', is a cry of anguish. In this way the reader is left with a narrow chink of hope: the indication that the German catastrophe should not have been, as well as the meagre comfort that a new beginning may be possible. Both novels reach out gropingly for a faint new dawn simply because they are laments:

> Wann wird aus letzter Hoffnungslosigkeit, ein Wunder, das über den Glauben geht, das Licht der Hoffnung tagen? Ein einsamer Mann faltet seine Hände und spricht: Gott sei euerer armen Seele gnädig, mein Freund, mein Vaterland (*14*, p.773).

Finally, the problem of interpretation is similar in both novels, though this is not to say that the style is the same. As usual Mann produces his own comments on this problem. On one occasion he has Adrian Leverkühn define music as 'die Zweideutigkeit als System' (*14*, p.74). Such a description has a particularly apt relevance for Mann's novel as a whole and equally for *Die Blechtrommel*. Elsewhere in *Doktor Faustus* Thomas Mann sympathises in effect with the predicament of the reader:

> Für den Nicht-Künstler ist es eine recht intrigierende Frage, wie ernst es dem Künstler mit dem ist, was ihm das Angelegentlich-Ernsteste sein sollte und zu sein scheint; wie ernst er sich selbst dabei nimmt und wieviel Verspieltheit, Mummschanz, höherer Jux dabei im Spiele ist (*14*, p.569).

As we have already seen in the course of this book, ambiguity, ambivalence, parody and irony present as many problems for the non-artist in *Die Blechtrommel* as they do in *Doktor Faustus*.

Thomas Mann and Günter Grass, those masters of parallelism, seem to invite the reader to compare *Doktor Faustus* and *Die Blechtrommel*: in so doing, he gains many intriguing and stimulating insights into both novels and realises at the same time how deeply Grass's novel is embedded in the German literary tradition.

Select Bibliography

1. Arnold, Heinz Ludwig, *Günter Grass, Text + Kritik*, 1/1a, 1978.
2. Booth, Wayne C., *The Rhetoric of Fiction* (Chicago and London, University of Chicago Press, 1961).
3. Bourrée, Manfred, 'Das Okular des Günter Grass', in Gert Loschütz (ed.), *Von Buch zu Buch — Günter Grass in der Kritik* (Neuwied and Berlin, Luchterhand, 1968).
4. Brode, Hanspeter, *Günter Grass*, Autorenbücher (Munich, Verlag C.H. Beck/Verlag Edition Text + Kritik, 1979).
5. ——, 'Die Zeitgeschichte in der "Blechtrommel" von Günter Grass. Entwurf eines textinternen Kommunikationsmodells', in Rolf Geißler, *Günter Grass Materialienbuch* (Darmstadt and Neuwied, Luchterhand, 1976).
6. Enzensberger, Hans Magnus, 'Wilhelm Meister, auf Blech getrommelt', in *Einzelheiten* (Frankfurt, Suhrkamp Verlag, 1962); also in Loschütz (see *3*); and in Schlöndorff (see *22*).
7. *Frankfurter Neue Presse*, 14 November 1959; referred to also in *23*, p.57.
8. Grass, Günter, 'Rückblick auf "Die Blechtrommel" oder der Autor als fragwürdiger Zeuge', in Schlöndorff (see *22*); also in Rolf Geißler (see *5*); and in Günter Grass, *Aufsätze zur Literatur* (Darmstadt and Neuwied, Luchterhand, 1980).
9. ——, *Über meinen Lehrer Döblin und andere Vorträge* (Berlin, Literarisches Colloquium, 1968); also in Günter Grass, *Aufsätze zur Literatur* (see *8*).
10. Hatfield, Henry, 'Günter Grass: the artist as satirist', in Robert R. Heitner (ed.), *The Contemporary Novel in German* (Austin and London, University of Texas Press, 1967), pp.117-34.
11. Hollington, Michael, *Günter Grass: The Writer in a Pluralist Society* (London and Boston, Marion Boyars, 1980).
11a. Jurgensen, Manfred, *Über Günter Grass, Untersuchungen zur sprach-bildlichen Rollenfunktion* (Berne and Munich, Francke Verlag, 1974).
12. Just, Georg, 'Die Appellstruktur der Blechtrommel', in Manfred Jurgensen, *Grass: Kritik — Thesen — Analysen* (Berne and Munich, Francke Verlag, 1973).
13. Leonard, Irène, *Günter Grass* (Edinburgh, Oliver and Boyd, 1974).
14. Mann, Thomas, *Doktor Faustus* (Stockholm, Bermann-Fischer Verlag, 1947).
15. Muecke, D.C., *Irony* (London, Methuen, 1970).

16. Neuhaus, Volker, *Günter Grass*, Sammlung Metzler (Stuttgart, J.B. Metzlersche Verlagsbuchhandlung, 1979).

17. ——, *Günter Grass: Die Blechtrommel* (Munich, R. Oldenbourg Verlag, 1982).

18. Pascal, Roy, *The German Novel* (Manchester, University Press, 1956).

19. Reddick, John, *The 'Danzig Trilogy' of Günter Grass* (London, Secker and Warburg, 1975).

20. Reed, T.J., *Thomas Mann: The Uses of Tradition* (Oxford, Clarendon Press, 1974).

21. Richter, Frank, *Die zerschlagene Wirklichkeit — Überlegungen zur Form der Danzig-Trilogie von Günter Grass* (Bonn, Bouvier Verlag Herbert Grundmann, 1977).

22. Schlöndorff, Volker, *'Die Blechtrommel', Tagebuch einer Verfilmung* (Darmstadt and Neuwied, Luchterhand, 1979).

23. Tank, Kurt Lothar, *Günter Grass* (Berlin, Colloquium Verlag, 1965).

24. Thomas, Noel, *The Narrative Works of Günter Grass, a Critical Interpretation* (Amsterdam/Philadelphia, John Benjamins Publishing Company, 1982).

25. Thomson, Philip, *The Grotesque* (London, Methuen, 1972).

26. Wellek, René, and Austin Warren, *Theory of Literature* (London, Cape, 1949).